Contents

Copyright: Judy Horacek 2006. *Make Cakes Not War*. Scribe Publications

INTRODUCTION
ABOUT THE BOOK

1

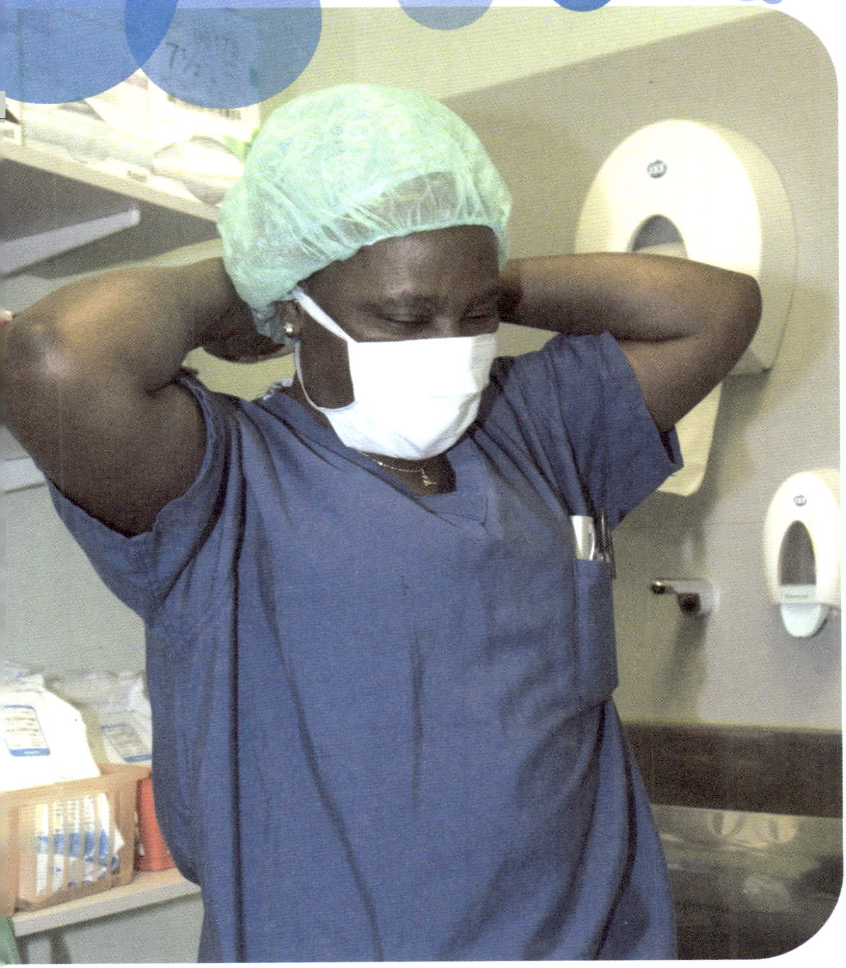

I. INTRODUCTION
About the book

ROADS to success

- Is a practical career-planning handbook for *all* foundation trainees (although medical students can use it as well).
- Provides a structured framework to help *all* foundation trainees with their post-foundation career planning (it is not just aimed at trainees who are having difficulty making up their minds).
- Includes exercises that have been tailor-written for junior doctors and that have been tried and tested over a number of years.
- Is based on a rigorous review of both the general career-planning literature and the specific literature on medical specialty choice.
- Aims to help foundation trainees make robust career decisions, and to know how best to implement their plans.
- Also contains guidance for educational supervisors, on how best to support trainees with the task of career planning.

How this book is organised

This book uses a structured four-stage approach to career planning:

Stage 1: Self-Assessment
Stage 2: Career Exploration
Stage 3: Decision Making
Stage 4: Plan Implementation

There are numerous reasons why this framework is used, but one vital benefit of the structured approach is that it helps you approach the task of career planning in a systematic way. To give you some examples, worrying about your application forms or interviews (Stage 4 activities) is a waste of time if you are not clear about Stages 1–3. Similarly, poor decision making (Stage 3) often rests on inadequate self-assessment or career exploration (i.e. Stages 1 and 2).

The importance of a structured approach was illustrated by a large-scale research study of work-based career discussions (Hirsh et al, 2001) which found that if the providers and recipients of career support shared a common framework, the recipients found the discussions more useful. So, in this handbook, while Chapters 2–5 are written for the foundation trainees, Chapter 6 is for the educational supervisor, enabling both parties to share such a framework.

(We would also recommend that both parties read the whole book. For example, Chapter 6 suggests questions, linked to the four stages, that educational supervisors might want to discuss with their trainees. In order to get the most out of these meetings, trainees might find it extremely helpful to look at these suggestions in Chapter 6 in advance, as a way of preparing for their educational appraisal.)

When this book was written

The first edition of ROADS was finished in April 2007. The current edition is being written exactly a year later. During this period there have been significant alterations to the details of post-foundation specialty recruitment. So information that is no longer applicable has been deleted from the current edition.

However, whilst the Tooke Inquiry into Modernising Medical Careers has reported its recommendations, and the government has responded to the recommendations, the precise details of specialty recruitment for 2009 and beyond have not yet been decided.

In the two chapters that are most affected by these changes (i.e. Chapter 3 which describes the career opportunities that are available post-foundation, and Chapter 5 which describes the application process) the content has been written in the knowledge that the detailed information may well change by January 2009, when the next major recruitment round into specialty training takes place. So, for example, detailed information about particular specialty pathways has not been included, as the 'shelf-life' of such information may well be very short. Instead, where relevant the reader is directed to other sources of information (e.g. MMC, deanery and Royal College websites), which will be up-dated regularly. In this way, the advice given in Chapters 3 and 5 will be applicable, even if the details of the system change.

But it is also important to stress that much of the important information included in Chapters 3 and 5 (e.g. how to research different opportunities; how to fill out the application form and prepare for interviews) applies even if the precise details of specialty recruitment change.

How to use this book

The exercises in this book can be used in different ways. You can complete them on your own, and then discuss your answers with colleagues, partner, family and, of course, your educational supervisor. In some trusts the exercises are also incorporated into structured foundation trainee career-planning sessions.

But whether you complete the exercises on your own, or as part of a workshop, we strongly advise you not to take a 'pick and mix' approach. Although it is tempting (particularly if you have decided on your post-foundation options) to skip Stages 1–3 and turn straight to Stage 4, this is not the most effective way to plan your career. Even if you know what you want to do post-foundation, the exercises within Stages 1 and 2, and the thoroughness of your decision making (Stage 3), will give you the raw data that you need to draw on for your application form and interview. Skipping straight to Stage 4 may reduce your chances of being successful in implementing your preferred career option.

About the title

Central to the book is the **ROADS** checklist. This provides a way of analysing your career decision, to see if it is robust. Specifically, when you have made up your mind about your post-foundation career, you should imagine that somebody is challenging you with the following questions:

Realistic: Are you being realistic about yourself *and* about the demands of the job?

Opportunities: Have you given serious consideration to all the opportunities available?

Anchors: Have you built in the things that provide support in your life?

Development: Does your decision adequately develop your potential?

Stress: Have you minimised those aspects of work that you find particularly stressful?

And in addition to posing these questions to yourself, we would also advise that you discuss your answers with your educational supervisor, or another experienced clinician.

About the authors

What experience do we bring to the task of writing this career handbook?

- Between the two of us we have been providing career support to individuals and groups for 30 years, working for commercial career consultancies and in our private practices.
- Both of us are qualified careers professionals and qualified users of psychometric tests.
- CE completed her Ph.D. in the Department of Academic Psychiatry at the then Middlesex Hospital and is a chartered psychologist. For the past nine years she has worked part-time as a deanery education adviser and spent hundreds of hours observing consultants teach their juniors in clinical settings. She has also run training workshops for trainees and/or consultants on career issues within KSS as well as for the Eastern, London, Oxford, and West Midlands deaneries.
- JR is currently working as a senior careers adviser for the South Thames Foundation Schools. She has provided career counselling and coaching to a wide range of professionals at a variety of stages in their careers.

But neither of us is clinically qualified, so in writing this book we have worked closely with senior clinicians, and also with medical students and foundation trainees. In this way, we hope that we have produced a practical handbook that will assist medical students and foundation trainees with the challenging task of planning their post-foundation careers.

STAGE 1 OF CAREER PLANNING
SELF-ASSESSMENT

II

II. STAGE 1 OF CAREER PLANNING: Self-Assessment

Overview

In this chapter, after a brief introduction, you will be introduced to three self-assessment exercises. These exercises cover:

- Work values
- Achievements/skills and interests
- Stresses and strains

There follows a description of different psychometric instruments. If you do decide that the psychometric approach might help you with your career decision making, then details of how to get yourself tested are included in this chapter. Finally, the chapter ends with two different approaches to summarising the results of the Stage 1 self-assessment activities.

Introduction: a clinical analogy

Although there are many different models of patient consultation, in some shape or form they will all cover taking a patient history, examining the patient, deciding whether further tests are necessary (and if they are, carrying them out), forming a diagnosis, implementing a treatment plan, and then reviewing progress. Furthermore, these tasks have to be carried out in the right order: if an unknown patient walked through the door of your consulting room you wouldn't recommend a specific treatment if you hadn't taken a history, examined him or her, perhaps carried out some further investigations, and formulated a diagnosis.

Models of clinical consultation can serve as a good parallel for a career-planning framework:

Patient consultation	**Career planning**
Taking patient history	Self-assessment
Examining the patient	Exploration of particular career options
Formulating a diagnosis	Career decision making
Implementing a treatment plan	Implementing a career plan

Significantly, in both clinical consultation and career planning, the first two stages are linked. What you have elicited during the patient history informs the focus of your clinical examination. Similarly, in terms of career planning, what you find out in Stage 1 (self-assessment) informs not only which different career options that you explore in greater detail, but also the specific issues that you research within each career option. For example, if you have realised that your core work values include great continuity of patient care and opportunities for teaching, part of your research would be to find out whether, in the career options that you are exploring, you would tend to care for patients over a long time-span and also have plenty of opportunities for teaching.

In both clinical consultation and career planning there might be a certain to-ing and fro-ing between the stages. So, for example, a clinical sign that is seen on examination might mean that you go back and ask further questions about the patient's current or past medical history; and while you are planning your career, something that you find out when you are researching a particular career option might lead you to go back and undertake some more self-assessment.

This parallel between clinical consultation and career planning is useful in that it highlights the importance of approaching both tasks in a systematic manner, and being guided by an underlying staged framework. However, we do want to stress that it is not a perfect parallel. In clinical consultation the aim (although it is not always realised) is to establish a definitive diagnosis – to provide an answer to the question: 'What is it that is causing these symptoms in this patient?' In terms of career planning, the notion of a definitive diagnosis can be unhelpful as it might be taken to suggest that each individual could only be happy in one particular specialty. This is counter to the wider research literature, which strongly suggests that individuals could be satisfied in a number of different career options.

A further problem with the parallel is that it might unwittingly seem to imply that there is something wrong with the person (they can't decide on their career), and so they need treatment (finding out about themselves and different options), to make them 'better'. Instead, as careers professionals we would argue that not only is it completely 'normal' for people to have difficulty deciding on their career options, but also the four-stage model that we have used in this book applies equally to people who are having difficulty deciding and to those who have already decided, but want to maximise their chances of success.

Stage 1: self-assessment

Adequate clinical decision making cannot occur if the doctor has taken a poor history, performed an examination inadequately or ordered the wrong clinical investigations. Similarly, in our respective career-counselling practices it is striking how often it is that clients who are dissatisfied with their previous career choices had leapt into their chosen lines of work with scant attention to what they were looking for in a job (self-assessment) and only cursory research into whether the job they were considering would match their particular career needs (career exploration).

Starting with self-assessment, there is a whole range of aspects of yourself that you could investigate, and for each of these there are different possible ways of carrying out the self-assessment. In this handbook we focus on three key areas: work values, skills/interests and the stresses/strains of work. We regard these as the bare minimum in terms of the range of issues that you need to consider when planning your career.

Personality instruments (such as the Myers-Briggs Type Indicator) or Interests/Personal Attributes Inventories (such as the Self-Directed Search or the Sci59 specialty choice inventory) are also being used to help medical students and trainee doctors with their career decision making. So we also provide some guidance on when psychometric testing might be appropriate and how best to interpret the results.

Exercise 1: work values

Introduction to exercise 1

Rob Nathan, a leading occupational psychologist and career counsellor, has written an excellent practical guide for career counsellors. In his book (Nathan and Hill, 2006), he has the following to say about work values:

> 'Values in relation to work represent the degree to which a person regards his or her work as worthwhile. This "worthwhileness" includes the amount of power, autonomy, creativity, learning, altruism, security, status and money which are sought in work.'

Clearly 'worthwhileness' is an important component of occupational satisfaction, and thus it is vital to become clearer on one's underlying work values.

The exercise below is adapted from a generic set of work values (Hobson and Scally, 2000). Using the experience gained from running workshops for trainees in four deaneries, we removed work values that participants felt were not relevant to medicine, and replaced them with values that the participants felt were missing from the generic list. In addition, there have been a small number of research studies on doctors' work values, and we checked the list that we had assembled against this research literature, to see that there was a reasonable fit.

We have also adapted Hobson and Scally's grading criteria, in the light of a trainee's comment that it is important to think about those work values that you *don't* want to be present. (And, in fact, this notion that occupational decision making also involves thinking about things that you *don't* want accords with the wider research literature.)

Work value cards

NOT IMPORTANT	**QUITE IMPORTANT**
IMPORTANT NOT PRESENT (i.e. important that you don't have this at work)	**VERY IMPORTANT**
PLACE OF WORK Working in a specific part of the country	**MONEY** The possibility of earning a high salary
VARIETY Having a variety of different responsibilities	**COMPETITIVE** Working in a specialty to which entry is highly competitive

INDEPENDENCE Being able to work on your own	**MANAGING YOUR OWN TIME** Having some flexibility in when you carry out your different responsibilities
FRIENDS Forming friendships with colleagues at work	**PACE OF WORK** A rapid pace of work
RESPECT A high-status job	**MANAGING OTHERS** The opportunity to manage a clinical service
CREATIVITY Thinking up new ideas and ways of doing things	**EXCITEMENT** Working in a context where you take clinical decisions under pressure
CONTACT WITH PATIENTS Working in a context where you have lots of contact with patients	**TECHNIQUES** Working in a specialty in which you perform particular surgical and/or diagnostic procedures
COMMUNITY SETTING Working in a community-based specialty	**HOSPITAL-BASED** Working in a hospital-based specialty
RECOGNITION Receiving appreciation for the work you do	**JOB SECURITY** Knowing that your work will always be there for you
CONTROLLABLE LIFESTYLE Working in a specialty where you can achieve a satisfactory work/life balance	**PRECISION** Working at tasks which involve great care and precision

CONTINUITY OF CARE Working in a specialty where you can provide continuity of care for your patients	**SUPERVISION** Having responsibility for supervising others
HELPING PEOPLE A role in which you help individuals, groups or society in some way	**LEARNING** A rapidly changing role in which you will continually be learning new things
BEING EXPERT Being known as someone with special knowledge or skills	**ORGANISATION** Working in a well-known hospital or service
PROMOTION Work in which there is a good chance of promotion	**CHALLENGE** Being 'stretched' and given new problems to work on
PREDICTABILITY Having a work routine which is fairly predictable	**RESEARCH** Having the opportunity to carry out research
COMMUNITY Working in a place where you can get involved in the local community	**WORK WITH OTHERS** Working in a team alongside others
PHYSICAL CHALLENGE Work that is physically demanding	**TEACHING** Being able to teach others
FLEXIBLE WORKING A role in which there is the possibility of working part-time	**TYPES OF PATIENTS** Working with a particular patient group

Instructions for Exercise 1

1. Photocopy this exercise. Then, using the photocopies, cut out the four 'headings' cards:

   - Very Important
   - Quite Important
   - Not Important
   - Important Not Present

2a. Again using the photocopies, cut out the individual work values cards. Then sort the work values cards under the four headings (i.e. pile up those work values that are 'Very Important' to you under the 'Very Important' heading, etc.)

2b. Try to be a little selective – so, for example, don't have more than seven or eight work values cards under the 'Very Important' heading.

2c. If there are any work values that are not on the list, but you know have a significant bearing on your career decision-making, then add them in on separate pieces of paper. (You can add them in under any of the four headings.)

2d. If you can, try to rank-order your 'Very Important' work values.

3. Write down your 'Very Important' work values. (And, if you have managed to rank them, write them down in rank order.)

1. ______________________	5. ______________________
2. ______________________	6. ______________________
3. ______________________	7. ______________________
4. ______________________	8. ______________________

Look at your list and consider the following questions:

a. Is there anything that surprises you, or anything that has raised your awareness about yourself from the list? If so, make a note of whatever it is that has struck you.

b. Think about how your work values might change over time. Are there any values which are not 'Very Important' now – but might be so in 5–10 years' time? ('Flexible working' may be an obvious one, but there might well be others.) If this is the case, then make sure that you take a note of how you imagine your work values might change.

c. Are there any work values which you regard as 'Very Important' but are unlikely to find an outlet in any of the options you are considering? (For example, artistic values are very important to some doctors, but they don't necessarily find an outlet for them in their paid role in medicine.) If this is the case, is there any way that you could find an outlet for these values outside work? And if you did, would this be satisfactory for you, or might you still end up feeling unfulfilled?

Exercise 2: achievements, skills and interests

Introduction to exercise 2

In this exercise we ask you to consider three achievements – two from your work as a junior doctor/medical student and one from outside work.

Typically, when we give trainees/students this particular exercise on courses, some will say that they don't actually have any achievements. But such a response is based on a crucial misunderstanding. When we say that we would like you to consider three achievements, we are not saying that they should be of world-shattering importance or enormous, or rare (e.g. a lead paper in a major medical journal). Instead, what we are asking you to identify is something that you have done that you felt proud about, and ideally, but not essentially, something for which you received positive feedback from a patient, colleague or supervisor.

It is also important, given that this exercise is part of the self-assessment stage of an overall career-planning model, that your answers are genuine, rather than of the 'Miss World/I'd like to save the planet' variety. The purpose of the exercise is to think about things that you have done well, and which have given you a glow of satisfaction. It is not about impressing others – but rather starting to think more clearly about what makes you tick, so that you can use this knowledge as the basis for subsequent career decision making.

Instructions for exercise 2

A. Read through your foundation portfolio and identify two things that you were involved with at work which gave you great personal satisfaction. When have you felt the glow of satisfaction that you did a particular task well? When have you received positive feedback?

(See if your foundation portfolio jogs your memory about particular achievements. But if it doesn't, choose something that you haven't written about in your portfolio. The vital thing is to choose something that you did well and you found personally satisfying).

If you are a medical student, you may have a learning portfolio that you could use for this activity. If you do not have either a medical student or foundation portfolio, then just choose something from your memory.

In addition to the work-based example you should also identify something that you have been involved with, out of work, that gave you great satisfaction. Possible examples include achievements in sports, music, drama, local community action, charities, religious institutions, etc. Sometimes, though, the 'out of work' achievements are home-based. For example, if you have got through medical school while simultaneously caring for a young child, then that is a very real achievement – and you can use it to demonstrate the possession of a whole range of personal skills such as commitment, organisation, time management, etc.

B. For each achievement, identify all the skills involved. These could be technical skills, communication skills, organisational skills, conceptual skills, etc. Tease out all the skills that you used to accomplish each of the listed achievements. Moreover, don't just list the broad type of skill (e.g. 'communication skills), but try to analyse your achievements at a more detailed level. (See the example below.)

C. For each achievement, describe how you (and, if possible, other people) knew the achievement was a success.

Example

<u>A. Achievement:</u>
Successfully presenting case at first multi-disciplinary case conference.

<u>B. Skills involved:</u>
Summarising complex case notes.
Building effective relationships with the other professionals present at the conference, none of whom I had met before.
Presentation skills – presenting my point of view to the other attendees.
Standing firm when my viewpoint was challenged, but not resorting to using a similarly confrontational approach.

<u>How did I (or other people) know it was a success?</u>
Feedback from other people attending the case conference.
Despite initial opposition, the care plan that I suggested was accepted by the team.

D. Finally, look at the lists of skills you have identified. Put a mark next to those skills that you are most interested in using at work. You can also note down the skills that you have not developed yet, but that you want to develop in the future.

Repeat the exercise for the other two achievements.

Exercise 3: stresses and strains

Introduction to exercise 3

Now switch your focus to areas in and out of work that you find difficult. All specialties will contain tasks that you enjoy less; however, good career decision making involves identifying what you find stressful and difficult, and then choosing a career pathway that minimises these particular stresses.

You might think that people do this automatically, and some do. However, we frequently encounter clients who have made choices based on one factor (e.g. family pressure), without adequately considering the way in which this choice will involve other factors that they find stressful.

Instructions for exercise 3

What we would like you to do in this exercise is to identify two examples (one from your working life and one from outside work) in which you felt that your stress levels were higher than they normally are for you.

Again, it may help you to read through your portfolio to jog your memory. For the non-work example, flick through your personal diary, to see if any examples come to mind.

Having identified the two examples (one from work, and one from outside work), then answer the following questions. (Go through them separately for each example).

1. Give a brief description of the situation, outlining the background, what role you played, and what feelings it engendered in you.
2. Try to identify what it was about this situation that made you feel the way that you did. For example, for the work-based scenario, was it the feedback from others, the pace of work, the response of the patients, etc.

3. What can you learn from this example in terms of factors that you might want to minimise at work?

Now repeat the exercise, this time analysing an example from outside work.

(And, of course, you can repeat this exercise, giving more than one work and one outside work example.)

Psychometric instruments

Psychometric instruments are sometimes used in career counselling to assess psychological attributes relevant to occupational choice, such as occupational interests, work values and personality.

What does 'instrument' mean in this context?

As doctors, the word 'instrument' conjures up images of the specialised equipment that surgeons use in theatre. But a psychologist uses the word somewhat differently. For a psychologist there is a difference between a psychometric test and a psychometric inventory, and therefore the generic term 'instrument' is used to describe something that applies to both tests and inventories.

To explain this in a bit more depth, for a psychologist, a psychometric 'test' refers to measures that assess *maximum performance*. The underlying assumption of these is that individuals will attempt to perform at the top of their form. So, for example, a psychometric assessment of verbal ability would be classified as a 'test', as people who filled it in would probably want to do as well as they possibly could. This can be contrasted with psychometric measures of *typical response*, which are often called inventories. These are based on self-report, with individuals describing their likes and dislikes, or how they typically behave.

The most common instruments that are used when career counselling doctors are measures of personality (such as the Myers-Briggs Type Indicator), or measures of personal attributes and professional preferences such as Sci59. These should therefore be called psychometric instruments or psychometric inventories, not tests, as they do not assess maximum performance. (See Kidd, 2006.)

But we appreciate that using the term 'instrument' in this way probably sounds strange to medically qualified readers.

What makes them psychometric?

Next it is important to consider what makes a set of questions 'psychometric'? After all, the three exercises given earlier in this chapter also aim to assess interests, and work values, and probably also relate to one's personality.

Without going into excessive detail, the most important point to make is that with a 'psychometric' instrument (as opposed to the sort of exercises included earlier on in this chapter) data are available on the measurement properties of the instrument – in particular, on its reliability and validity.

Taking each of these in turn, the reliability of an instrument refers to the extent to which the instrument produces stable results (assuming that the underlying psychological construct that the instrument is trying to measure hasn't changed). The validity of the instrument refers to whether the instrument actually measures what it purports to be measuring, so, for example, a measure of occupational interests should actually assess that construct and not some other one.

Both these concepts should be familiar to you from your study of clinical diagnostic tests, but in a clinical context they may be given different terms. For example, instead of the term 'reliability' you might have seen the terms 'precision' or 'reproducibility', and instead of the term 'validity' you might be more familiar with the concept of 'accuracy'.

But despite the conceptual overlap, there are also some subtle differences between clinical diagnostic measurements and the measurement of psychological constructs (i.e. psychometrics). In a clinical situation accuracy can be defined as the relationship between test results and 'gold standard' results, where the latter refers to an independent definitive diagnosis of the presence or absence of disease. In at least some clinical situations, the 'gold standard' actually exists, which in turn underpins the measurement of diagnostic accuracy. Things are never so well defined with psychometrics, where the 'gold standard' (of intelligence, interests, values, etc.) is always another theoretical construct rather than having the more clear-cut status of a particular clinical diagnosis. And we think it important to bear this difference in mind, when you are considering taking a psychometric instrument to help you with your career decision making.

When might psychometric instruments be helpful?

Let's return to the analogy between clinical consultation and career decision making. While most initial consultations are likely to include taking a clinical history and clinical examination, it is not always the case that further clinical investigations are necessary.

As qualified test users we would suggest that a similar situation applies to the use of psychometric instruments in helping medical students/junior doctors with their career decision making. The self-assessment exercises and strategies for career exploration included in this book will probably be sufficient for many (perhaps even the majority) of students/trainees, and they will be able to make career decisions without recourse to psychometric instruments.

However, some students or trainees get a bit stuck. They struggle with the self-assessment exercises, or having carried out the self-assessment exercises don't know how to translate the results of the exercises into ideas about which specialties to explore. For these trainees, personality inventories or measures of occupational interest can, if used appropriately, be helpful.

But it is really important to introduce some words of caution, and for you to understand what psychometric instruments can and cannot tell you.

Introducing another analogy might help make the position clearer.

As qualified (or nearly qualified) clinicians, you may well have been irritated by ill-informed accounts of medical issues that you have read in the popular press, or heard discussed in social situations. You know about the importance of an evidence-based approach with representative samples, appropriate clinical-outcome measures, adequate time-scales to measure the effects, etc.

Similarly, as experienced careers practitioners, we are often alarmed (and, if we are honest, sometimes infuriated) by the ill-informed pronouncements that are made about the role of different psychometric instruments in helping medical students and trainee doctors with specialty choice. We know about the importance of examining the psychometric properties of the instrument (i.e. the reliability and validity), and critically appraising the evidence that this particular instrument might be an accurate predictor of future satisfaction in different specialties.

So. What is the evidence?

Personality inventories

Personality measures attempt to cast light on our individual temperaments – to what extent we are for example cautious, adventurous, curious, gregarious, competitive, independent or sociable. These types of characteristics may have an impact on the kind of work that we do well and enjoy and also on the type of work tasks or environments that we might enjoy less, and find more difficult to carry out.

In terms of evaluating the evidence on the relationship between personality and medical specialty choice, the picture is complicated by the fact that different measures of personality have been used with different groups, thus making comparisons extremely difficult. Furthermore, some of the studies were carried out 20 or even 30 years ago and there may have been considerable shifts in the nature of a particular specialty during that period. And as most of the data comes from the USA rather than the UK, given that there are differences in the organisation of healthcare in the two countries, it is possible that the way in which a particular specialty is practised in the two countries may also differ significantly. So this too would complicate the picture.

However, the most recent review of the literature (see Borges and Savickas, 2002) concluded the following:

- Although there is a loose relation between a few personality factors and particular medical specialties, there is more variation in personality traits *within* medical specialties than *between* them.
- All personality types appear in all specialties.
- More than one medical specialty fits the personality of any particular medical student.

But on the basis of this, the authors do not in fact conclude that personality testing has no place in career counselling medical students or trainee doctors. Instead, they recommend that personality instruments should be used as a way of increasing self-knowledge, rather than as a diagnostic process that will 'match' a particular personality to a particular specialty. A narrowly diagnostic approach is not supported by the available evidence, and should be avoided at all costs.

What this means in practice is that if you complete a questionnaire such as the Myers-Briggs Type Indicator (MBTI), you cannot use it to identify the specialty to which you would be best suited. But you can use it to find out a bit more about yourself, and then use that increased self-knowledge (in addition to the self-knowledge gained from the other activities outlined in this handbook) to think creatively about specialties that might suit you.

Accessing the MBTI

Nowadays it is possible to access the MBTI online, and a quick internet search will identify a list of organisations that provide this service. However, as the potential benefit of the psychometric approach resides in the quality of the feedback discussion, we would not recommend you going down this route. Instead, Appendix A gives a list of professional bodies that accredit career counsellors, and the information in Appendix A about the British Psychological Society explains how you can identify a suitably qualified individual who would administer the MBTI, provide you with a report, and discuss the implications of the report with you.

Measures of occupational interests

Holland's Self-Directed Search is the most widely used measure of occupational interest. And the conclusion reached above about the use of personality instruments applies to the use of the Self-Directed Search. (See Borges et al, 2004.)

In this later paper, Borges et al make the following statement in their conclusion:

> 'Early in their training medical students should be disabused of the idea that there is one perfect specialty choice for each person. Instead they should be helped to understand how they could use different specialties to construct satisfying and successful careers.'

Given that the MMC changes mean that trainees now need to make career decisions earlier on in their careers, and also that they can opt to apply for basic specialty training in up to four different basic specialty programmes, it seems that they should derive some comfort from these findings. (And for the cynics among you, it is perhaps worth stressing that these findings were based on studies in the USA, so it is not a political coincidence that such data became available just as the foundation pilots were being devised!)

Sci59 (previously called Sci45)

Finally, there is our own home-grown UK inventory, Sci59. This instrument was developed to measure personal attributes and professional preferences of doctors in training and beyond and to match these to the characteristics needed to prosper in the 59 most common specialties, including general practice.

As a relatively recent 'kid on the block', Sci59 was not included in either of the two studies listed above. However, the basic notion that *all* psychometric instruments should be used to suggest career ideas and increase self-understanding, rather than to 'diagnose' what specialty will suit you, is a basic tenet of sound career-counselling practice, and thus applies to Sci59.

In addition, it has to be stressed that there are no published predictive validity data on Sci59 (or on its earlier version, Sci45). What this means is that there are no published studies that have attempted to correlate Sci45 scores with any measure of occupational satisfaction of people in post. (And, in fact, while the original list of items was drawn from interviews with consultants and GP principals, in drawing up the final list of items Sci45 was actually calibrated using responses from SHOs who had not yet embarked on their specialty training.)

As for the practicalities, some medical schools and deaneries have made Sci59 available, while others have not. At the time of writing (April 2007), it is not yet available for individual medical students or doctors to purchase themselves, although it may be at some point in the future. So if you are interested in taking Sci59 you need to contact your personal tutor or Foundation Programme manager, to see if it is on offer locally.

Conclusions

We cannot stress strongly enough that psychometric instruments that are included as part of a career-planning process need to be regarded as tools that lead to greater self-awareness rather than as simple quick-fix solutions.

But people like certainty. And if you are in the highly stressful position of trying to choose your next career move, you might be desperately seeking answers. So you don't necessarily want to hear that psychometric instruments are indicative rather than diagnostic, and can't actually provide you with definitive solutions.

Given that you may well be desperate for an answer, feedback should always be given by people who understand what the test can and cannot tell you, and know how to use the results to enhance self-understanding.

Ultimately, what you will get out of any additional instruments is highly dependent upon the skills of the person who is giving you feedback. If they challenge you to think about the ways in which the results of the instrument accord (or don't accord) with your other self-assessment activities, and if they are all too aware of what the instruments can and cannot tell you, then it can be useful. If not, then it is at best useless, and, at worst, misleading.

Summary of Stage 1

Introduction to summary

It is now time to construct a summary of Stage 1. (Remember that the process of carrying out the career exploration tasks in Stage 2 might make you reconsider some of your answers to these Stage 1 exercises. Therefore it is perfectly acceptable for you to return to and refine this Stage 1 summary at a later date.)

Read through your answers to the Stage 1 exercises that you have completed. If you have completed any psychometric instruments, then read through the report summaries, as well, at this point. Then record the key points using the summary headings given below.

1. The doctor–patient relationship

(Write down any points that have emerged from the Stage 1 exercises relating to the doctor–patient relationship. These might include some or all of the points listed below, but you can also add your own personal points. The list below is not necessarily exhaustive.)

Do you want to see patients in a community or hospital setting?

Do you enjoy brief encounters with patients, or providing continuity of care over long periods of time?

Do you want to spend most of your working day having contact with patients?

Do you want to work with acutely ill or chronically ill patients?

What about the emotional landscape? (For example, do you find it rewarding to work with patients who are in a distressed or disturbed emotional state?)

Do you have preferences about the ages of your patients? And do you prefer working with individual patients, or patients and their families?

Do you want to contribute directly to the treatment of patients, or would you enjoy working to support the diagnostic process (e.g. in areas such as diagnostic radiology or pathology)?

Would you enjoy having to consider the whole of the patient's body (e.g. GP/paediatrician), or would you enjoy becoming an expert on a specific region of the body (e.g. ophthalmology)?

Do you enjoy performing technical diagnostic or interventional procedures?

2. Intellectual matters

(Some of these issues might have emerged in the earlier Stage 1 exercises, but it is possible that they have not. If they haven't, it doesn't matter – just fill out the summary now.)

What areas of academic work have you most enjoyed studying in your undergraduate and postgraduate training?

What medical journals are you most drawn to reading?

Within the *BMJ*, what sorts of articles tend to attract your attention?

What subjects have you enjoyed (or might you in future enjoy) teaching to others?

What subjects have you enjoyed (or might you enjoy in future) carrying out research on?

What subjects have you carried out an audit on (or might you plan to carry out an audit on in future)?

3. Status

In this section in particular (although it actually applies throughout the whole of this Stage 1 summary), it is important to ask yourself whether your answers represent your own views, or whether you are being unduly influenced by pressure from significant others, such as parents or partner.

How important is it to you that you work in a highly competitive branch of the medical profession?

How important is status to you?

Do you want to ensure that there are opportunities for private practice in your chosen specialty?

Do you want to go into a branch of medicine where there is the potential for earning a very high salary?

Is it important to you that you have opportunities for participating in research?

Are opportunities for travelling abroad with your work important to you?

4. Quality of life

What sort of work–life balance do you want to have in 5–10 years' time?

What sort of weekly schedule would you like to have in 5–10 years' time?

What, for you, are your core work values, from which you derive most satisfaction?

What stressful factors do you want to minimise at work?

Is the length of postgraduate training an issue for you?

5. Relationships with colleagues

Do you want to be able to spend quite a portion of your day working on your own?

Do you want to be able to spend quite a portion of your day working in teams?

Do you enjoy working in multi-disciplinary teams?

Do you want to be able to develop and manage a clinical service?

Do you want to be able to do quite a lot of teaching?

Do you want to be able to carry out research?

An alternative way of summarising Stage 1

Instructions for alternative summary

Some people prefer diagrams and pictures to words. If you would prefer, you could provide a more visually based summary of Stage 1.

Take a large piece of paper (either A3 or paper from a flipchart).

Copy out the outline of the shield shown overleaf.

Then, in each of the four quadrants, either write bullet points of the key issues or, if you are so inclined, you can devise symbols to depict the key issues.

Then, underneath the shield, you could write a brief punchy motto that encapsulates what it is that is important to you in your work.

The example on the following page, was provided by a consultant in general geriatric medicine.

Figure 1: Shield and motto from a consultant

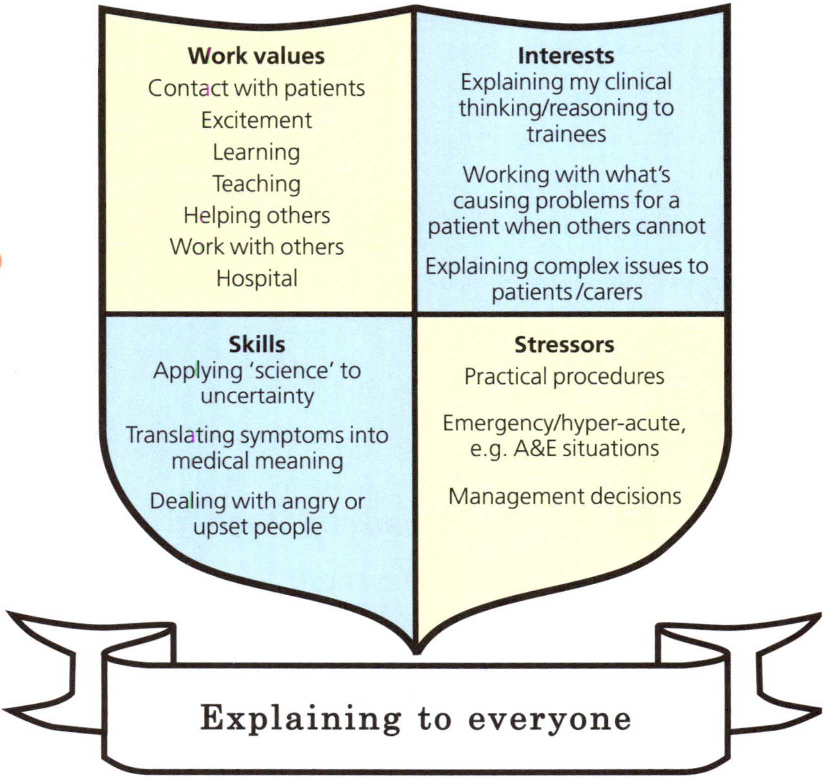

Final comments

Hopefully you have found these exercises useful. But if you haven't, we would ask you to bear with us.

When you come to apply for jobs, completing the Stage 1 exercises in sufficient detail will help you construct clear, credible answers on your written application forms, and also help you prepare how to answer the sorts of questions that will be posed at interview. This is because the quality of your career decision making will be thoroughly scrutinised in the application process, and you need to demonstrate that you have carried out adequate self-assessment (Stage 1), and thorough career exploration (Stage 2).

STAGE 2 OF CAREER PLANNING
CAREER EXPLORATION

III

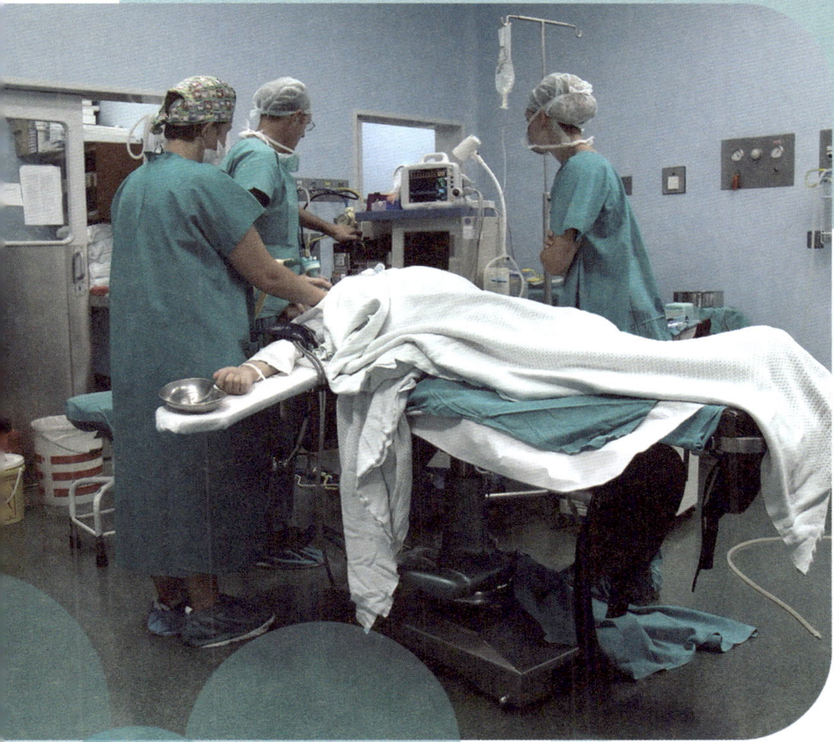

III. STAGE 2: Career Exploration

Overview

This chapter covers Stage 2, career exploration, in detail. After a brief explanation of why this stage is so important, the structure of post-foundation training is outlined. You will then be introduced to preliminary research tasks that you can carry out for a number of different career options, and more detailed research tasks that you will carry out on a smaller sub-set of options. Advice is also given on how to narrow down your options, so that you know which options to research in greater depth. The chapter ends with a 'reality check' so that you give sufficient thought to whether or not your career choices are realistic.

Why Stage 2 matters

The exercises covered in Stage 1 should have given you an opportunity to develop a clearer idea of what you are looking for in your career.

In Stage 2 you explore different career options, in order to find out two things: Firstly, you need to research different options in order to establish which particular career pathways are most likely to match your own individual skills, interests, values, personality, etc. Secondly, given the feedback that you have received from people such as your educational supervisor, clinical supervisor, the trust Clinical Tutor/Director of Medical Education or the Foundation Programme Training Director, you need to consider whether the option (or options) that you are interested in seem to be realistic career choices.

At the beginning of Stage 2 we want to stress that adequate career exploration takes time. But it is time well spent. (Both of us have worked with many clients who never really explored their career options properly, and then, over a period of time, came to regret their earlier choices.) In addition, as we described above, spending time exploring different career options is not only important in terms of making good career decisions, but will also help you later on at the application form and interview stages.

We also want to emphasise that Stage 2 is not carried out in a vacuum – but, rather, Stage 2 follows on from Stage 1. This means that as well as finding out the basic 'facts' about a particular career choice (and by this we mean factors such as typical training pathway, person specification, competitiveness, etc.), you will also need to research the specific questions that you now realise (on the basis of working through Stage 1) are important to you.

An easy way of doing this is to use the summary exercise that you completed at the end of Stage 1 to generate specific issues that you are going to explore in your specialties of interest.

A couple of other points stem from this idea that Stages 1 and 2 are linked:

Firstly, the clearer you are about what is important to you (Stage 1), the more targeted and relevant your Stage 2 research is likely to be.

Secondly, a lot of the more personalised information that you need to find out about is not available in the various medical career handbooks or on the websites of the different Royal Colleges and deaneries. Instead, in order to find out what it is 'really really' like to work in a particular specialty, you will need to talk to people who are currently working in that particular field. Without this sort of research (called 'informational interviewing' in the career-counselling world), it is difficult to ascertain whether the career is going to match your core work values, skills, interests, etc.

Post-foundation training

The first edition of this book was finished in April 2007 and described the post-foundation system that was in place at that time. A year on, a modified system is in place. The Tooke Inquiry into MMC was published in January 2008. At the point of writing this second edition, the Department of Health's response to these recommendations have also been published, but details of the structure of post-foundation training that will be in place for January 2009 have not yet been finalised.

If you want to pursue training in a particular specialty (including General Practice) you will need to apply for a specialty training post. In 2008 (in comparison to 2007) most specialties used a locally led (i.e. deanery led) recruitment and selection system. Also unlike the initial proposals for 2007 in which it was planned that there would be only one recruitment process per year, currently there is staggered recruitment with specialties organising up to three recruitment rounds in a year.

In a deanery led system each deanery organises their own recruitment process i.e. the deanery is responsible for advertising the vacancies, devising their own or specialty-based structured application form with specialty specific questions, working out their own shortlisting criteria and scoring systems (based on nationally agreed person specifications) interviewing and selecting successful applicants; making offers and receiving acceptances.

In contrast to the majority of specialties that are using locally based systems, some specialties in 2008 are recruiting by means of a national process. These specialties include small specialties with small numbers of vacancies nationally (e.g. cardiothoracic surgery and plastic surgery amongst others). In addition, some larger specialties for which shortlisting and interview processes and scoring systems across the country have already been standardised are also using a national recruitment process. Specialties which fall into this category include Paediatrics and Child Health; Obstetrics and Gynaecology and General Practice. Finally, Academic Clinical Fellowships are using a national recruitment process.

Run-through and un-coupling

A 'run-through' programme is one that offers the trainee a structured training package that will take them through (assuming satisfactory progress) to the point where they can be awarded a Certificate of Completion of Training (CCT). Any applicant who was offered and accepted a 'run-through' training post in 2007 will continue to have run-through training, as long as they demonstrate satisfactory progress in each year of their training.

Some specialties have continued to offer run-through training programmes in 2008. These include Obstetrics and Gynaecology, Paediatrics and Child Health and General Practice.

In those specialties which are offering run-through training in 2008, there will also be some fixed term specialty training appointments (FTSTAs) on offer. This will mean that there are some opportunities for doctors to develop their training experience so that they might be successful at a later date in securing a specialty training post. But it has to be recognised that in many specialties there will be high levels of competition and taking a FTSTA in a highly competitive specialty won't in any way guarantee later success in obtaining a training post at ST2 or 3.

In contrast to those specialties that are still offering run-through training plus some additional FTSTAs, in 2008 a number of specialties have 'un-coupled'. What this means is that instead of offering a run-through training programme, these specialties will offer a two-year post-foundation core training (CT) programme (three years for psychiatry and emergency care) followed by open competition to enter specialty training in future years at ST3 onwards (ST4 for psychiatry and emergency care, as the core training lasts three years). In other words, securing a core training post does not guarantee your progression through to CCT. You will have to go through another round of competition for posts at the end of your core training.

Entry for posts at this junction between core training and higher specialty training will be open to all eligible applicants (including those working in non-training posts or otherwise not on core training programmes). This means that there may be some opportunities in future years to enter training at a higher level, for those people who were not previously successful in securing a core training post. But again, in highly competitive specialties, it is likely to be extremely difficult for an applicant to secure a training post at ST3/4, if they have not previously been in a core training programme.

And in future years?

It is not possible to provide details of the recruitment and selection processes that will be used by particular specialties in 2009 – let alone beyond that. However, it is possible to make some general comments that should stand the test of time.

1. Keep on top of the system.

Post-foundation training is in a considerable state of flux and the only way that you can ensure that you are not disadvantaged by failing to find out about critical information is to carry out regular checks of three different types of websites:

a. Deanery websites, of any deaneries to which you might apply

b. Royal College websites, of any specialties to which you might apply

c. The Modernising Medical Careers website which produces key documents outlining and updating details of post-foundation training

2. Begin early

Don't leave your career exploration to the last minute. This has never been a wise strategy but in the current system of flux it is particularly unwise. Instead, from the time you start in your first foundation post you should be regularly carrying out the self-assessment tasks described in the previous chapter, and the career exploration tasks described in this chapter.

3. If you are uncertain – ask for help

As a foundation trainee you will have an educational supervisor, as well as access to other senior clinicians with additional educational responsibilities such as the Director of Medical Education or College Tutor. If you are unsure about the implication of what you read on these different websites (or in the medical press), then ask for clarification from one of these people. It is known that the system is particularly confusing at the moment, and it is better to seek clarification early on, rather than wait until the point when everybody is filling in their application forms.

Preliminary research tasks

The sorts of issues that you might want to begin by researching (and in fact you may carry out this more basic desk-bound research for a number of different options) include the following:

Entry criteria to the specialty: this is clearly laid out in the person specifications which are available on the MMC website. You can then review your Stage 1 assessments against the person specification, to see if there is a close fit, or if there are any skills or experiences that you might need to acquire.

If you are not currently on a foundation programme, you need to check that you are applying for entry to the correct level. Your educational supervisor or Clinical Tutor should be able to advise you on this. Alternatively you can contact the careers specialists at your deanery. If you have a very unusual query, you can also email the MMC help desk: support@mmc.nhs.uk

The applicant's guide to Specialty Training (available on the MMC website) contains detailed advice for overseas applicants, and it is important that all overseas applicants read this information carefully before submitting an application. And if you have any queries the careers specialists at your deanery or the MMC help desk (see above) should be able to help. Currently (April 2008) a detailed consultation is taking place on the issue of managing medical migration.

This consultation will finish in May 2008, and it is not possible to predict what guidelines will be in place in 2009 or beyond. It is therefore important that all overseas applicants check the MMC website regularly, so they keep up to date with any changes to the law.

The C word (Competition)

In the past it was very difficult to get information about the relative competitiveness of different specialties. One of the deaneries (the West Midlands) pioneered the production of data on the comparative competitiveness of different specialties, but these were local rather than national figures. National data from the previous round of recruitment are now available (typically on MMC documents) and it is important that you familiarise yourself with this information. You also need to discuss the possible implications of the competitiveness of your specialty choices with your educational supervisor.

Beyond preliminary research

Some of you may know immediately which options you want to explore further. If this applies to you then skip to the next section. But others of you may be far less sure.

If you fall into this latter category (i.e. you don't know which options to explore in depth), then the following suggestions might help:

1. Complete a relevant psychometric instrument in order to generate lists of specialties that might suit you. (Remember, though, that in the previous chapter it was argued in some detail that results from psychometric instruments should never be regarded as narrowly diagnostic.)

2. Discuss your Stage 1 summary with your educational supervisor, clinical supervisor, the Clinical Tutor/Director of Medical Education or the Foundation Programme Training Director, to see if they can help you with ideas of careers to which you might be suited.

3. Read through one of the specialised medical career handbooks mentioned in Appendix B. From this, choose a number of career options that seem, on initial reading, to be interesting.

4. Search through the *BMJ Careers* website which contain numerous articles on careers in different specialities.

5. Check the websites of the different deaneries. Many of them have good basic descriptions of the different specialties (including General Practice).

Isn't there another way of identifying suitable careers?

Perhaps you are surprised that there isn't a more 'scientific' method than the suggestions listed above. But based on our professional training, and also on our experience of helping people make good career decisions, we know that this process is as much an art as it is a science. So called 'scientific' approaches (particularly the use of psychometric instruments) can be useful in generating ideas, but they don't hold all the answers. And often the answers start to emerge through following up the suggestions of colleagues and supervisors with whom you have worked, coupled with a fair smattering of background reading.

And finally – if you have done all of the above – and nothing grabs your attention, perhaps you need to ask yourself whether you actually want to remain in medicine. If this is the case, we strongly recommend that you either ask for a referral to the specialist careers adviser (if your Deanery has one), or you seek out some private career counselling with an appropriately qualified careers counsellor. (See Appendix A for a list of organisations that accredit careers professionals.)

How to research options in further depth

Having decided which options you wish to explore further, you then need to work out what it is you wish to find out, and how you will go about doing so.

Often, the best way to find out more about a particular career option is to try it out, as one of your foundation programme placements. But if this is not possible (either because the specialty you are interested in doesn't offer foundation placements, or because you weren't successful in getting the placement you wanted), then see if you can arrange a 'taster' week ideally early in your foundation year two. A good place to start would be to discuss this with your educational supervisor and Foundation Programme Training Director.

Informational interviewing

Look at the summary you constructed at the end of Stage 1. For each of the five different sections, write down a list of specific questions that you are going to ask of the person who is (or people who are) currently working in the options that you are interested in.

You then need to identify at least one person (and preferably more than one) working in that specialty, in order to put these questions to them. Ask your educational supervisor for suggestions as to whom you can ask. In addition, you can approach college tutors. It is helpful if you are able to talk to people at different levels of seniority, so ask among your friends to see if they know SpRs or consultants working in your field of interest.

Finally, set yourself a suitable timescale in which these interviews will be carried out and arrange to discuss your findings with your educational supervisor, or other experienced clinician.

Person, phone or email?

Ideally you should talk to people face to face. (And some Deaneries organise careers fairs where you can talk to people in all sorts of different specialties, and the BMJ Careers Fairs are also useful ways of talking to people in particular specialties.)

Clearly if you are doing a foundation placement in a large teaching hospital you will have easier access to a broader range of specialties than if you are in a specialised psychiatric hospital or a smaller District General Hospital. If you can't manage a face-to-face interview, then see if you can arrange to talk to somebody on the phone.

And if all else fails – email people, and ask if you can send them a list of questions.

But whatever your mode of communication, you need to approach the task of informational interviewing as an important research project. You are not having an aimless 'chat'; instead, you are trying to get answers to some of the questions that have emerged from the Stage 1 self-assessment.

(Be aware that some of the responses to questions will be quite subjective Therefore it is useful to speak to more than one person. Find out what the interviewee enjoys about their work. Not only is this interesting information to elicit, but if they give you a very cynical response, then you know that you might be getting a somewhat jaded opinion. And while it is clearly important to get a balanced rather than an overly glossy view of the specialty, you do want to avoid being turned off a specialty because you have talked to a burnt-out clinician.)

Finally, it's worthwhile going back to the library and spending a bit of time with your nose in the journals. Choose the major journals in your specialty of interest (if you are unsure about which journals these are, ask the librarian) and spend some time having a good read through some recent issues.

Of course, as you haven't begun specialist training in these areas, many of the articles will be too specialised. But, in general, ask yourself whether you are gripped by some of the articles, or whether they leave you somewhat cold.

In addition to the relevant journals, you can also ask the librarian to direct you to some of the core texts in the fields that you are exploring. And again, pose yourself the same question. Am I really interested in reading more about psychiatry (cardiology, pathology, etc.)? Because if you are, that is a good sign. But if you are not (assuming that you have chosen a textbook at approximately the right level), then you need to ask yourself whether you are making a good career decision.

Reality check: is your career decision realistic?

This is probably the trickiest issue of all.

During courses for consultants we often get asked about the best ways of approaching trainees who have 'an insight by-pass'. And the consultants then start to give detailed descriptions of trainees with severe dyspraxia who want to train in micro-surgery.

But, on the other hand, I also often hear from consultants who had been advised at an earlier stage of their career that 'they would never make it' as a radiologist, gastro-enterologist, etc. And there they are, 15 years into their careers as consultant radiologists or gastro-enterologists. If they had listened to the 'advice' that had been given to them earlier on, they would have perhaps denied themselves the chance of succeeding in the career that they had set their hearts on.

As a trainee, you have to ask your educational supervisor whether they think that your career plans are realistic. (And if your educational supervisor knows little about the specialty you are considering, then, having completed some of the career exploration tasks, you should be able to fill them in with details of the person specification, training pathway, competition ratios etc.)

Clearly if they feel that your plans are realistic, then there isn't a particular problem. (Although in the current climate of flux you should realise that this support from your educational supervisor doesn't in any way guarantee that your plans will be successful.)

But if your educational supervisor thinks that you are not being realistic, then you are in a more sticky position, and you should always try to get as much information as possible as to the specific nature of their concerns.

If you think that there has been a breakdown of communication with your educational supervisor and that you have been unfairly judged, then you can ask to discuss your plans with another consultant, or with the Foundation Programme Training Director. (In the final chapter, we will recommend to all clinicians who may be taking part in these sorts of 'second opinion' meetings that they always have a copy of all the previous assessments and also a brief report from the educational supervisor.) But, by all means, ask if you can have a 'second opinion' from another clinician.

Perhaps you feel that your difficulties in a certain placement were due to things going on in your personal life, and you are confident that you could have performed better if circumstances had been different. If at all possible, discuss this with your educational supervisor or Foundation Programme Training Director. But, if you feel unable to do so, then this will be something that you take account of, but remains concealed from your supervising consultants.

Ultimately the decision as to what to put down on your application form is your own. And if you decide that your educational supervisor is being unfair or unduly pessimistic, then you can of course act against their advice. But we would urge you, at the very least, to respond to any comments that you get about not being realistic – by saying to yourself: 'How do I know that it is realistic given the feedback that I have received?' And you should also ask yourself: 'How am I going to be able to convince the short-listing panel and interviewing panel that I am a suitable candidate?' To avoid challenging yourself with these two questions is to adopt the ostrich approach. And, as yet, there aren't too many ostriches in senior medical positions.

Copyright: Judy Horacek 2006. *Make Cakes Not War*. Scribe Publications

STAGE 3 OF CAREER PLANNING DECISION MAKING IV

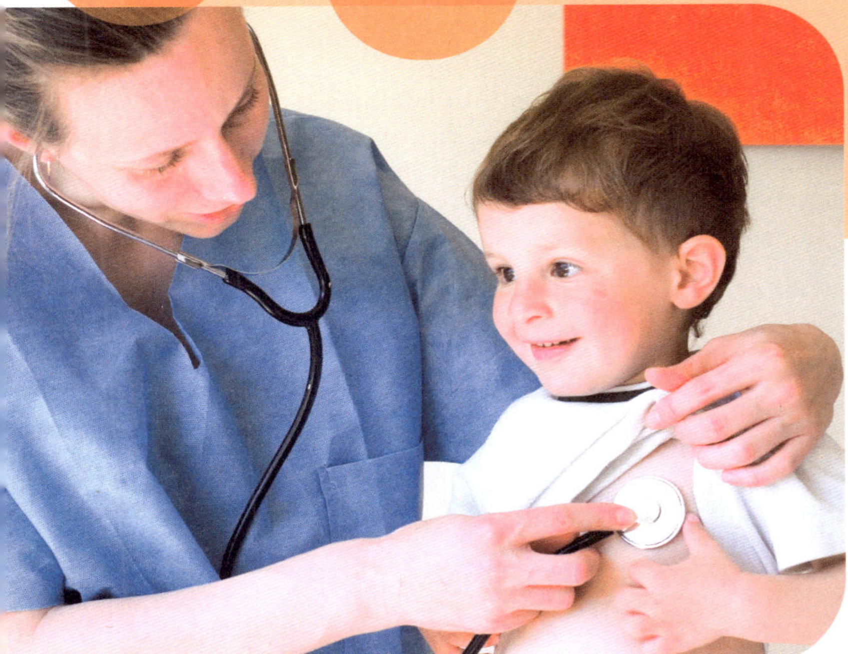

IV. STAGE 3 OF CAREER PLANNING: Decision Making

Overview

This chapter guides you through the decision-making process.

There are three exercises in this chapter. The first ('Constructing a Lifeline') provides you with an opportunity to review significant decisions that you have made in the past. The second ('The Decision Template') offers a structured approach for comparing the different options that you are currently considering.

But whatever method you use, by the end of Stage 3 you will need to have reached a decision about which option (or options) you will be applying for next.

The third exercise involves you using the ROADS acronym to check the robustness of your career decision, and the chapter ends with brief advice for those of you who are finding it difficult to make up your mind.

Exercise 1: constructing a Lifeline

Instructions for exercise 1

Think about how you have made important decisions in the past: for example, career-related decisions about A-level subjects, applying for medical school, elective choices, etc., or personal decisions that are unrelated to work, such as taking a gap year between school and university, starting or ending a significant personal relationship, etc.

Then, follow the instructions below. (And see Fig. 2 for an example.)

1. Take a sheet of paper (ideally A3 or flip-chart paper. But A4 will work if it is all that is available). Turn it round so that it is 'landscape' rather than 'portrait'.

2. Draw a horizontal line across the middle of the paper. Note down your age at the right-hand end of the line. Then, put in a 'plus' (+) above the horizontal line (to signify times that you look back on with pleasure) and a 'minus' (-) below the line (to signify those times when things were not going well).

3. Before you go any further, think very carefully about the course the line will take. Where are the high points and the low points? Which parts of the line (if any) are relatively stable?

4. Now mark in the significant life events. Include experiences which influenced you, achievements, and both good and bad events that have occurred in your life to date. Allow yourself sufficient space, as including one event may trigger a memory of another.

5. Connect up the points that you have marked.

6. Identify a couple of decisions that you have marked on your Lifeline which you feel (in retrospect) have worked out well. What made them good decisions? How did you go about making these particular decisions?

7. Now, identify a couple of decisions on your lifeline that you feel (in retrospect) didn't work out so well.* What made them poorer decisions? How did you approach these decisions that didn't work out so well?

8. A much-favoured adage of psychologists is that the best predictor of future behaviour is past behaviour. Bearing this in mind, can you use this analysis of past decisions to throw any light on how you should approach the career choices that you are currently facing?

   (One way of doing this is to look at your answers to questions 6 and 7 in order to identify the best way for you to approach your current decision, as well as approaches you should avoid. For example, do you seem to be somebody who makes good decisions when you rely on your 'gut' feelings, or are you

---

**When we have used the Lifeline exercise in workshops (with both consultants and trainees), we have often heard the comment that there is no such thing as an entirely 'bad' decision, as good elements can emerge even from decisions that didn't turn out at all smoothly. We would both entirely agree with this, and have examples from our own personal career histories that illustrate the point. Moreover, in our professional practice we often hear clients describe career decisions that they regret taking, but which they do realise also allowed them to develop certain useful skills.*

However, in terms of the Lifeline exercise, we do think that it is possible to identify decisions that you have taken that, in retrospect, you feel were not the best ones. These are decisions where, even though you can see that some good things have emerged from them, you have a sense that a different decision at that point in your life would probably have been a better option. It is these sorts of decisions that we would like you to identify in question 7.

somebody who has made your best decisions when you adopt a more structured approach?)

9. Has anything else struck you from completing this Lifeline exercise?

   (And in case you don't understand this question, it might help if we give you an example of the sort of insight that can emerge. One of us once ran a two-day career-planning workshop for a housing association that was making a large number of staff redundant. The staff attending the workshop were, for entirely understandable reasons, angry, de-motivated and anxious about the future. One particular member of staff was very withdrawn during the first day of the workshop, and was reluctant to contribute to the discussions, or complete any of the activities. Following the Lifeline exercise, there was a noticeable shift in his attitude. When the facilitator remarked on this, and enquired what had happened, the member of staff replied that he had felt overwhelmed by the forthcoming redundancy, and had convinced himself that he wouldn't get a new job. But when he reviewed his lifeline as a whole he realised that the current dilemma was just one of a series of obstacles that he had faced in his life and, as he had overcome the previous ones, he now felt more confident that he wouldn't be defeated by the forthcoming redundancy. This is just one example. But it gives a flavour of the sort of insights that sometimes emerge from the Lifeline exercise.)

Figure 2: Lifeline example from a consultant

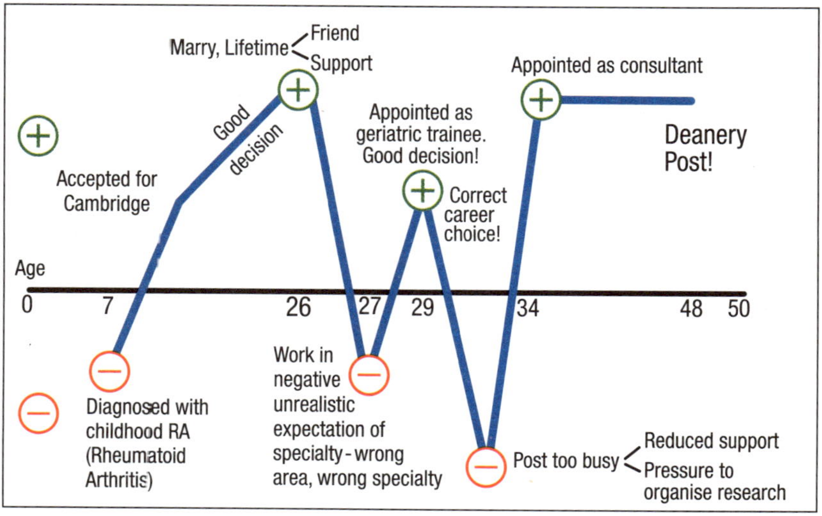

Exercise 2: a more structured approach to decision making

Instructions for Exercise 2

If the results from the Lifeline exercise suggest that you would benefit from a more structured approach, then you might find the exercise below helpful.

1. With reference to the Stage 1 Summary, and using the five headings (Doctor–Patient Relationship, Intellectual Matters, Status, Quality of Life and Relationships with Colleagues), write down the factors that are key to you achieving personal satisfaction at work (see Fig. 3).

   Then, along the top, write down the particular career options that you are currently considering. (Ideally, this should not be more than four, as otherwise the decision making becomes rather unwieldy.)

2. With reference to your Stage 2 research, note down whether the key factors are present or absent for each of the different options that you are currently considering. (See Fig. 3 – it includes the areas we identified in Stage 1. You may wish to add extra questions as a result of your Stage 1 exercises and you can add more columns to consider more options.)

3. Counting the number of 'ticks' in each career option may well be misleading, because the different factors are not necessarily of equal importance. Instead, we would suggest that initially you 'eyeball' the chart, and see what conclusions you reach. Having done that, we would recommend that you discuss the chart with significant people in your life (partner, family, close friends), and also with your educational supervisor, or another clinician who knows your clinical work.

   In this way, the best career decision should become clearer to you.

   In this exercise we haven't included the precise details of how many options you have to choose from at any particular stage (i.e. the details of application for foundation year 1 or post-foundation training). We cannot gaze into a crystal ball and predict the precise details of the application process into foundation year 1, or into post-foundation training that will be in place next year, let alone the year after. Thus we took the decision to describe a generic approach to decision making which can be applied to any situation.

Figure 3: Exercise 2 – Questions to consider for each option

Aspects of work

1. Doctor–patient relationship	Options (please tick)		
	1	2	3
Do you want to see patients in a community or hospital setting?			
Do you enjoy brief encounters with patients, or providing continuity of care over long periods of time?			
Do you want to spend most of your working day having contact with patients?			
Do you want to work with acutely ill or chronically ill patients?			
What about the emotional landscape? (For example, do you find it rewarding working with patients who are in a distressed or disturbed emotional state?).			
Do you have preferences about the ages of your patients? And do you prefer working with individual patients, or patients and their families?			
Do you want to contribute directly to the treatment of patients, or would you enjoy working to support the diagnostic process (e.g. in areas such as diagnostic radiology or pathology)?			
Would you enjoy having to consider the whole of the patient's body, (e.g. as a GP/paediatrician), or would you enjoy becoming an expert on a specific region of the body (e.g. ophthalmology)?			
Do you enjoy performing technical diagnostic or interventional procedures?			

2. Intellectual matters	Options (please tick)		
	1	2	3
What areas of academic work have you most enjoyed studying in your undergraduate and postgraduate training?			
What medical journals are you most drawn to reading?			
Within the *BMJ*, what sorts of articles tend to attract your attention?			
What subjects have you enjoyed (or might you in future enjoy) teaching to others?			
What subjects have you enjoyed (or might you enjoy in future) carrying out research on?			
What subjects have you carried out an audit on (or might you plan to carry out an audit on in the future)?			

3. Status	Options (please tick)		
	1	2	3
How important is it to you that you work in a highly competitive branch of the medical profession?			
How important is status to you?			
Do you want to ensure that there are opportunities for private practice in your chosen specialty?			
Do you want to go into a branch of medicine where there is the potential for earning a very high salary?			
Is it important to you that you have opportunities for participating in research?			
Are opportunities for travelling abroad with your work important to you?			

4. Quality of life	Options (please tick)		
	1	2	3
What sort of work–life balance do you want to have in 5–10 years' time?			
What sort of weekly schedule would you like to have in 5–10 years' time?			
What, for you, are your core work values, from which you derive most satisfaction?			
What stressful factors do you want to minimise at work?			
Is the length of post-graduate training an issue for you?			

5. Relationships with colleagues	Options (please tick)		
	1	2	3
Do you want to be able to spend quite a portion of your day working on your own?			
Do you want to be able to spend quite a portion of your day working in teams?			
Do you enjoy working in multi-disciplinary teams?			
Do you want to be able to develop and manage a clinical service?			
Do you want to be able to do quite a lot of teaching?			
Do you want to be able to carry out research?			

Exercise 3: how robust is your career decision?

The final task that we would encourage you to complete is to interrogate your career decision using the ROADS criteria. Initially we would suggest that you should do this on your own. But then you should talk through your conclusions with the same people listed above. (And, of course, the results of all three exercises detailed in this chapter could be discussed with the relevant people on one occasion, or on separate occasions, depending upon your own particular circumstances.)

Good career decisions: ROADS

Realistic – are you being realistic about yourself AND the demands of the job?

Opportunities – have you given serious consideration to all the opportunities available?

Anchors – have you built in the things that provide support in your life?

Development – do your choices fully develop your potential?

Stress – have you considered those aspects of work that create particular stresses for you?

If you can't make up your mind

There are a number of possible reasons why you might struggle with a decision. (And in fact, these reasons are not mutually exclusive.)

1. You are still unclear about your skills, interests, achievements, values, etc.

2. Your career research to date hasn't enabled you to become more clear about the extent of the 'match' between the work factors that are most important to you and the different career options that you are currently considering.

3. Points 1 and 2 don't apply, but you still can't make up your mind (perhaps because you always struggle with decisions).

4. You are uncertain whether you wish to remain in medicine at all.

If 1 and/or 2 apply to you, and you haven't really devoted much time to working through the structured exercises outlined in this handbook, then it might be useful for you to go back and do so. But if you have completed the exercises to the best of your ability (or if 3 applies), then we would advise you to ask for a referral to the deanery careers adviser.

And if 4 applies, then we would strongly recommend that you seek professional help from an experienced and appropriately qualified careers professional (see Appendix A). Both of us have experience of working with individuals who fall into this category, and as a result we know that the decision to leave medicine is a major one, and that the individuals concerned have enormously appreciated the input from people who have a professional grounding in career planning.

Some final thoughts

A number of clinical colleagues have given us their insights into the decisions they made on their specialty choice – see Table 2 below.

Table 2: specialty choice – some reflections from three consultants and a GP

'I am a geriatrician. Like most of us, I think I made my decision quite late as I realised that I liked general medicine and didn't really want to specialise. I was also very aware of a work–life balance. I think I would have been happy in most specialties – most of us enjoy having specialist knowledge and being able to make a difference.'

'When I commenced my PRHO year, I had been quite determined to become a surgeon. During my stint in surgery, this interest strangely ebbed and disappeared, perhaps out of a realisation that I did not possess the appropriate mindset. I then considered paediatrics, which I had enjoyed as a medical student, but had concerns with pursuing, having had little personal experience of dealing with children. Two weeks as a PRHO in paediatrics proved sufficient to rekindle this interest and any anxieties were dissipated by paediatric trainees, who advised me to trust natural paternal instincts! Twenty-six years on, I have no regrets whatsoever.'

'You may want to use my quote as an example of how not to do it. I applied for chest medicine in the early 1980s for two reasons. Firstly, I and my contemporaries were assured that there would be lots of jobs in chest medicine in the late 1980s, when all the chest physicians appointed shortly after World War II to sanatoria posts would be retiring, and, secondly, I thought that my father, who died in my first year at medical school, was a chest physician and I wanted to follow in his footsteps. The sanatoria were closed down in the mid-1980s, and so jobs were extremely scarce in the late 1980s, and it turned out that my father was a cardiologist!'

Continued overleaf

'I made my specialty choice largely on the basis of work–life balance. I wanted a career that in the future would be flexible enough to fit around having children and possibly moving around the country (depending on my husband's work). This sounds quite old-fashioned and unambitious, but having subsequently gone on to be involved in running the GP Flexible Career Scheme, I know it is something a large proportion of female (and some male) doctors aspire to once the reality of having children hits home. It is very hard when choosing a career path in your mid-20s to think ahead to having a family, but I would encourage anyone who wants to do so (and has a partner with a career) to talk to as many doctors as they can who have attempted to combine career and family. I suspect many wish they could work part-time, but have been unable to do so in hospital specialties. As a GP you maintain ultimate responsibility for the care of the whole patient and the role has endless variety and stimulation. It is sometimes possible to negotiate a contract for "school hours only" for a few years, which is invaluable if you have small children and a partner who works long hours.

There are also many opportunities for outside interests; I have been able to develop a career as a GP educationalist while my children are still young, doing much of my work in the evenings when they are in bed and fitting the rest around school runs, sports days and all the rest of family life. It was definitely the right choice for me.'

Copyright: Judy Horacek 2006.
Make Cakes Not War.
Scribe Publications

STAGE 4: PLAN IMPLEMENTATION

V

V. STAGE 4: Plan Implementation

Overview

This chapter covers the nitty-gritty of putting your plan into action. It begins with a description of the application process, and then includes detailed advice on how to fill in application forms. In addition, CV guidelines are included in Appendix C. The chapter then moves on to explaining preparation you can do in advance of the interview, and also covers advice on performing well on the day. Although at the time of writing interview presentations for post-foundation posts were unusual, we don't know what will happen in the future, so some basic guidelines on giving an interview presentation are included in Appendix D.

The chapter ends by taking you right back to the beginning of the career-planning process, as it is argued that the task of career planning is not so much a linear process, but rather a reflective cycle. As such, it is something that you will need to engage in throughout the whole of your professional life as a doctor.

Application forms

In recent years there has been an enormous shift in the application process. Not so many years ago applicants filled in a standard hospital application form (which was often the same for administrative, clerical and all healthcare staff), and they also included a CV. In the old system very little weight was attached to the brief 'personal statement' on the standard application form, and everything went on the CV.

But times have changed, and currently there is a move towards structured application forms. One of the difficulties in this change is that some consultants haven't quite registered it. This means that they might not always provide the most useful advice. It is likely that application forms will continue to evolve and short-listing will probably still take place on the basis of some sort of structured application form. So thinking about how best to approach these forms is still a necessary task.

Initial preparation

Although in the current system you don't have to complete the application in one sitting, it still helps if you are thoroughly prepared for when the application process goes live.

One useful way of making the task of filling in these forms easier is to prepare an up-to-date CV in advance (see Appendix C). This means that all the background data (dates of exams, of electives, of different posts, etc.), is well organised in advance, and in one place.

In terms of helping you answer the more discursive questions on the forms, the answers to the exercises that you have completed in this handbook should provide good raw data. In addition, foundation trainees will also need to refer to their learning portfolios, while some medical students will have similar collections of reflective writing that they had to fill in for their undergraduate course. The better organised you are with these three documents (i.e. your CV, your answers to the ROADS exercises and your learning portfolio), the easier you will find the task of filling in the application form.

Overview of the application process

As described in the previous chapter, in 2008 most specialties used a deanery-led recruitment process, although some had national recruitment. What this means is that you have to familiarise yourself with the deanery, specialty and MMC websites, in order to be on-top of the process used in the specialties to which you intend to apply. If you look at these websites you will find out where the posts are advertised. In addition, you will also find out about the timeline for applications. These dates are immutable and you want to be aware of them well in advance, so that filling out your application forms doesn't become a horrendous last-minute rush. This is particularly important if you intend to submit a number of different applications.

In 2008 there was a detailed applicant's guide available on the MMC website and it is highly unlikely that a comparable guide will not be produced each year, to assist applicants with the process. You need to make sure that you have read through this guide and thought about its implications as soon as it is made available on the MMC website.

Figure 4: Overview of the application process for foundation and specialty training programmes

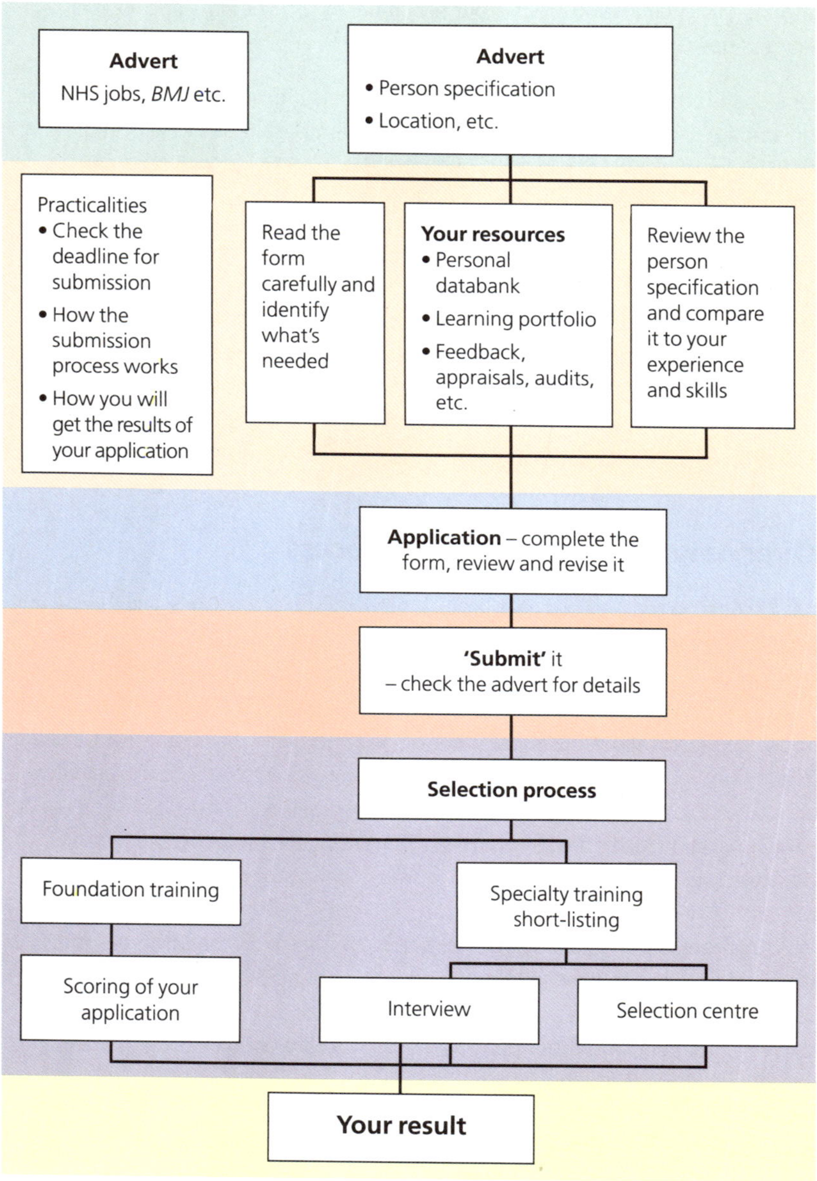

Some golden rules

Many of the points listed below will seem obvious. But one of us has had experience scoring applications for foundation programmes (and the other has considerable experience of medical recruitment and selection, particularly at consultant level) – and both of us know that a number of applicants disregard some of these basic points.

1. Preparation, preparation, preparation

Make sure that you understand the practicalities of the application process. This involves reading through the *whole* form extremely carefully. When is the deadline? Looking at all the questions, how long might it take you to devise really good answers? Will you need to find additional information that you don't yet have to hand?

You shouldn't start answering any question until you have studied the whole form, because an example that you give for one question might be one that you find you want to re-use for a subsequent question.

2. Understand what the recruiters are looking for

Familiarise yourself with the person specification for the training post as short-listing will take place with reference to this specification. (After all, you might bake the best chocolate chip cookies on the planet, but if the recruiters aren't looking for chocolate chip cookie bakers it probably won't do you any good to say so.) You always have to construct your answers to the questions with the person specification in mind. (But this doesn't mean a simple reiteration of the person specification on your application form. That approach becomes extremely tiresome for the reader.)

3. Check, check, and then check again

Mistakes (in spelling or grammar) will make it harder for you to get your points across and can lead to the loss of marks. You might feel that this is unfair as you are applying to work as a doctor, not an English teacher. But we would counter-argue that the difference between 0.25 and 0.025 mg for a particular medication could be a matter of life and death. Attention to detail matters, and being sloppy on your form won't help you get your message across.

4. A note about plagiarism

There have been a number of cases recently where applicants have been referred to the GMC for plagiarism. So bear in mind the guidance given in 'Good Medical Practice' that: 'You must be honest and trustworthy when writing reports, and when completing or signing forms, reports and other documents.' It also goes on to say that: 'You must always be honest about your experience, qualifications and positions, particularly when applying for posts.'

Completed application forms will be checked for plagiarism and the answers on the form must be your own rather than copied from the works of others. Using a commercial service to provide answers for your forms would not be regarded as compatible with the requirement that you write the answers yourself. And if the commercial services end up with a number of applicants writing very similar answers, then this is the sort of situation that might be detected by the anti-plagiarism software.

The issue of how much help friends/supervisors can responsibly give you is a far greyer area. But in Chapter 6 (the chapter for educational supervisors) we advise consultants to give you general feedback rather than mentioning specific wording that you should include on the forms.

How to approach the short-answer questions

There will be a number of questions on the form that relate to the person specification. You could, for example, be asked about your experience of team-working, leadership, time-management, making difficult decisions, or your longer-term career plans.

Typically, the space to answer these questions is limited to a specific word count.

Some consultants may be relatively unfamiliar with these sorts of questions, and may struggle with giving you the best advice. (Certainly, the advice that you can dash off any old answer, because these questions aren't that important, is not advice that you should follow.)

1. As a way of *preparing* to write your answer, you might want to use the STAR structure. By this we mean you could break down your example into:

   Situation/**T**ask
   Provide a concise overview of the example you are considering using, ensuring that it is relevant to the question.

Actions
What exactly did you do? What was your role and contribution? What skills did you use? (This part will probably form the bulk of your answer.)

Results/**R**eflection
What was the outcome? What have you learnt from it?

The STAR acronym is a very useful way of analysing the examples that you intend using in the short-answer questions.

However, depending upon the actual wording of the question, you might not actually include all the different parts, or you may want to emphasise one part more than another. So in the actual answer you will have to tailor the STAR components to the specifics of the question. But STAR is an excellent starting point.

2. As mentioned above, gather together all the relevant personal data that you might need to refer to, in one place, before you start answering these questions. And by this we mean your answers to the exercises in this book, your CV, your learning portfolio, information on any audits you have done and, for foundation trainees, the assessments that you have carried out.

3. Before you start writing anything, read through the GMC's guide 'Good Medical Practice' (which can be obtained from the GMC website). This will remind you of the qualities and values that the reader will be looking for in your answers. Scoring of the application form may relate to the elements of good practice outlined in this document.

4. Read the question extremely carefully. You need to make sure that you answer all parts of the question, as each part will be allocated separate marks.

   If the question has a number of parts, structure your answer in a logical way so that it matches the different parts of the question. In this way you will make it easier for the short-lister to recognise that you have fully answered all the parts. In addition, your answers always need to be relevant to the question that has been asked.

   (When we are running seminars on application forms we often say that you should imagine that each word you write is fighting for inclusion in your answer. If it doesn't 'add value', it shouldn't be there.)

5. When the question asks for examples of achievements, or initiative, or leadership, it is not requiring you to have extraordinary examples. In other words, the short-listers are not expecting you to have written the lead article in *Nature*, or have climbed to the top of Everest. Instead, they are looking for answers in which you reflect intelligently, and with insight, on the sorts of experiences that you would be expected to have, at your particular level of training.

6. You will find it easier to write good answers about generic skills (e.g. time-management, communication skills, team-working) if you have had some background training in these issues. If sessions on these topics are offered as part of the generic training programme, we would strongly advise you to attend them. This will give you a basic theoretical underpinning that you can use to structure your answer. If these sessions haven't been offered (or if you missed them), then do a bit of background reading before filling out the form.

7. When you are constructing your answers try to think about what an observer would notice if they had been watching you. For example, if you were asked to explain how you communicated with an agitated patient, a good answer might describe how you remained calm, and responded to the specific concerns the patient raised. If the patient had demanded to see the consultant, you would also explain carefully to the patient that the consultant was not on site, but you would be doing a ward round the following morning and take personal responsibility for asking him/her to speak to the patient when s/he was on the ward. An answer like this demonstrates to the reader that you do in fact know what constitutes effective communication with an agitated patient. In contrast, an answer which said something like 'I made sure that the way I responded to the patient diminished their level of agitation' doesn't convey to the reader that you would have the first clue how to do this in practice.

8. You will probably need to edit your first attempt at writing these answers. We suggest this because often the first draft misses points out, or includes irrelevant detail, but it is difficult to spot this at the time. Instead, if you write the first draft, and then leave it (for at least a few hours), when you come back to it, it is far easier to see what changes need to be made.

9. What you need to avoid is something that reads like a reiteration of the person specification. In contrast, what you want to aim for is something that engages the interest of the reader. With the best application forms not only is it clear that the candidate has the necessary abilities and skills, but the reader also builds up an initial sense of what the candidate is like as a person. It's a very hard balance to strike because you don't want to sound too confident or over-familiar. But you also don't want your answers to be arid or to sound as if they have come out of a textbook.

   In our experience the best way of finding the middle road and writing answers that engage the interest of the reader (and are, of course, also highly relevant to the question) is to write about examples that matter to you. With these examples, it is easier to convey your interest and involvement, and in turn this helps to engage the reader. But you also need to allow sufficient time for filling in the application form. If you have read the question carefully, chosen your most appropriate examples, and then fine-tuned your answers through sufficient editing, you are maximising your chances of success.

So how long is long enough?

There are no hard and fast rules on how long it takes to fill in your application form. But in our experience it usually takes longer than you would think.

We would certainly advise you not to leave the forms to the last couple of days before the deadline. Instead, look at them as soon as the system goes live, and approach filling them in in the systematic way that we have described above. It might also be helpful to ask more senior colleagues who have already completed these forms how long it took.

CVs

In 2008 CV based application forms, as opposed to CVs on their own, were used for specialty recruitment. However, as CVs form a useful way of organising data about your educational/career history to date, and as they may play a larger role in subsequent recruitment episodes, we have included some advice on writing CVs in Appendix C.

Interviews

Introduction

It is useful to begin by thinking about the purpose of interviews.

A formal answer is that the purpose of the interview is to assess each candidate against the person specification, and thus identify which candidate (or candidates) is best suited to the position on offer. But it is also important to realise that you (as the applicant) and the panel members all share membership of the human race. An interview should not feel like a mechanised process of quality control but, instead, a professional conversation in which you build up rapport with the panel.

Of course, building up such rapport is easier said than done. And nearly everybody is nervous before an interview – particularly when there is a lot at stake. But it is useful to remember that you want to convey a sense of who you are as a person during the interview. After all, the panel will be asking themselves if you are the sort of person whom they would want to have as a trainee.

If you are very nervous, it is fine to say to the panel that you find interviews quite stressful. Similarly, if you are asked an extremely difficult question you can begin your answer by saying something like 'That's a tough one. But I'll give it a go.' In these – and other ways – you can convey something of your personality to the panel.

We often remind our clients that interviews for jobs are not like police interrogations. By this we mean that whereas, if the police were interviewing you to find out if you had committed a crime, you would be unwise to comment that a question was very hard, or that you needed a bit of time to prepare an answer, such strategies are entirely appropriate in a job interview. Because, in the latter situation, responding in this way both gives a sense of your own personality and also shows that you handle pressure well.

Preparing for an interview

Most interviews will be structured and time-limited. There will almost certainly be more than one person present. If there is a panel, one member will be appointed as Chair, and is the person who is likely to welcome you, introduce the other panel members, and outline the structure of the interview.

If the mantra for estate agents is 'location, location, location', a similar refrain for career counsellors would be 'preparation, preparation, preparation'. (And this applies, of course, as discussed above, to the application form stage as well as to interviews.)

The reason why this is so important is that many questions can *broadly* be predicted in advance. So if you devote adequate time to pre-interview preparation, you should be able to improve the quality of your performance on the day. (Of course, you might still be asked some questions that you haven't considered before. But if a structured interview process is used, at least you can reassure yourself that all the candidates will have been asked this particular question.)

So how should you prepare?

For starters it is helpful to realise that questions which are asked at interviews are usually divided into three broad areas:

1. Questions about you.
2. Questions about the job/specialty.
3. Questions about the wider context of healthcare.

Each of these three categories will be considered in turn.

1. Questions about you

The list below gives examples of the sorts of questions about yourself that you might be asked.

1. Describe some of your key qualities/characteristics.
2. Tell me what you have gained from your training to date?
3. What are your key strengths?
4. What do you think is your greatest achievement to date?
5. Tell me about your approach to working in a team.
6. Describe a situation at work which, in retrospect, you think you could have handled better. What did you learn from the situation?
7. What sort of decisions do you find it difficult to make?
8. What do you see yourself doing in five years' time?

General guidance on these questions

It is always far better to refer to specific examples than to talk in generalities. So, for example, if you are asked about your strengths, mention perhaps two to four points, but link each of them to a specific example (which can be from work or from out of work). If you just talk in generalities (I'm compassionate, organised, thorough, etc.), a little voice pipes up in the head of the listener saying, 'Well, you would say that, wouldn't you?' But if you supply the examples, the answer as a whole has much more credibility.

(And as an aside: that's why working through the exercises in this book is important, because they supply you with the sorts of examples that you will need to draw on in your application forms and at interview.)

Not only should you have thought out examples of all your positive points, but you should also have planned what examples you will give if you are asked about your mistakes or areas of weakness.

The key thing to consider when you are asked about mistakes or areas of weakness is to choose an appropriate example. Bearing in mind the elements of the GMC's 'The New Doctor' you cannot refer to any example that would cause the panel to have doubts about your suitability as a doctor. But, equally, you don't want to refer to anything too trivial, or to be too clever by sneaking in a positive under the guise of a negative. For example, if you are asked about your weaknesses, responding by saying that you work too hard might be off-putting for the panel. Everybody has areas of personal weakness, and they should be able to discuss them, with insight, at an interview.

We would suggest that the best strategy is to choose a middle-of-the-road sort of example, and then – whether you are asked for this part or not – tell the panel how you remedied the situation. So, for example, you could say something such as initially you found it hard to switch off from work, and it was affecting your sleep. But you realised that you had to be able to recharge your batteries at the end of the day, so you started going for a run, playing the piano, reading a novel, or whatever, and that helped you to switch off from work and get a good night's sleep. (This is only one example – there are hundreds that you could use. But it illustrates the point that you need to pick the everyday sorts of examples that will have actually happened to you as part of your medical school/foundation training, and then describe to the panel what you did to remedy the situation.)

2. Questions about the job/specialty

Questions in this category might include the following:

1. Why do you want this job?
2. Why have you applied to this particular training programme?
3. Talk us through your CV.
4. What skills will you bring to this specialty?
5. Describe your views on whether less than full-time training is possible?
6. What do you think it takes to excel in this particular specialty?
7. What's the most useful course that you have attended in the last 12 months?
8. Tell us about a research paper that you have read recently that has had an impact on your clinical practice.

For questions of this type you will be drawing on your answers to the Stage 1 and Stage 2 exercises, including any psychometric instruments that you have completed. If you have given sufficient thought to both these stages you should be able to give coherent answers to these sorts of questions. This is because, essentially, most of these questions are assessing the match between your personal qualities and the demands of the job.

Before you go for an interview you should be familiar with the person specification, and any other basic information on training issued by the relevant Royal College. In addition, you should also try to get some sense (either through College literature or through talking to people in post) of likely developments in that specialty, because, with the introduction of new technologies, some specialties can expect significant changes in the future. (A well-known example is cardio-thoracic surgery, where the rise in invasive cardiology – performed by medically trained cardiologists, not surgeons – has meant that more procedures are being done through catheters, with earlier intervention in acute myocardial infarction, and therefore less open-chest surgery is required.) So check for likely future developments in your specialty of interest.

As for good ways of answering questions about the specialty, you need to distinguish between questions of different sorts. For example, if you are asked why you want to train in a particular specialty, you shouldn't have to pause for a long time before you answer. In fact, you should *expect* to be asked why you are applying for the post, and a good, well thought-out answer should be on the tip of your tongue.

However, you might also be asked to discuss some more complex scenarios related to your specialty – or indeed to the practice of medicine in general. In this situation, you will not be expected to have an answer immediately and it is perfectly acceptable to pause before you respond. (More detailed guidance on answering questions of this sort will be given below.)

Questions about the wider context of healthcare

Typical questions in this third category include the following:

1. What do you think about the recommendations of the Tooke Inquiry into MMC, and the Department of Health's response to these recommendations?
2. Describe how you think appraisal will help improve the quality of care that doctors deliver to their patients?
3. What do you think are the main challenges facing the NHS? (These could include Payment by Results, MMC, NHS Direct, Foundation Trusts, etc.)
4. Should patients be involved in decision making about their care?
5. How might the European Working Time Directive affect you?
6. What is audit, and how does it differ from research?
7. Can you tell me about an audit project that has influenced your practice?

In answering these questions you are not expected to be an expert on health policy or have an MBA in healthcare management. However, you are expected to have a basic understanding of the wider healthcare context in which you would be training.

As a basic minimum you should look at the following websites:

1. The Department of Health.
2. The relevant Royal College.
3. The Deanery/Foundation School to which you are applying.
4. The MMC website

In addition, you might also want to look through the on-line archives of *BMJ Careers* (to find recent articles about your specialty), *Health Service Journal* (to get short articles on health service topics) and perhaps even the King's Fund (which has good coverage of relevant NHS policy issues such as the establishment of foundation trusts).

If you are very keen on management issues, and see yourself as somebody who might want to manage a clinical service in future, see if you can get to talk to somebody in your Trust (or PCT) who has a senior management position. They will be able to give you a feel for how initiatives which you read about (e.g. Payment by Results) are being implemented in practice.

Questions that you can't easily anticipate

You might find that you are given particular clinical scenarios and asked to comment on them. Or, alternatively, you might be asked about your views on tricky ethical dilemmas.

As mentioned above, don't rush into answering questions of this sort, and take a moment or two to gather your thoughts.

As regards the clinical scenarios, the panel will be interested in both the content of your answer and also whether you demonstrate a systematic, well thought-out approach to the problem. If there is one fact that you are unsure about, then acknowledge this to the panel, but try your best to provide a logical, well-reasoned answer that demonstrates an ability to distinguish between essential and non-essential clinical tasks.

In contrast to the clinical scenario, if you are posed a complex ethical dilemma, you don't necessarily need to give the panel a hard-and-fast answer as to exactly what you would do. Instead, you can say that that is a very tricky situation, and one that you would hope that you would never find yourself in. In effect, you describe the factors that you would take into consideration when approaching the situation, rather than necessarily coming up with something cut and dried.

(If, though, the panel says that you are sitting on the fence, and they need you to be more explicit in what you would do, then of course you would have to come down on one side of the fence or the other.)

Structuring your answer

In the section above on application forms, it was suggested that you could use the STAR approach as initial preparation for your application form answers.

To recap: the STAR approach suggests that you should do the following:

1. Briefly describe the situation or task.
2. Briefly describe your own actions/activities – i.e. what you did.
3. Briefly describe the results (and/or your reflections).
4. The MMC website.

It can be useful interview preparation if you read through your portfolio, and the answers to the Stage 1 and 2 exercises, in order to analyse both positive and negative examples, using the STAR structure. However, we would not suggest that you necessarily stick to the STAR structure in how you word your answer in interview – or that you necessarily give equal weight to the different components. You certainly don't want to give the impression that you are parrotting pre-prepared answers, as this is unlikely to build rapport with the panel.

Instead, by thinking through clear examples (of both positive and negative aspects of your work) prior to the interview, you can give more succinct and focused answers.

General advice on interview technique

1. If you are being interviewed by a panel you need to make sure that you build rapport with all the panel members. Although you should focus your eye contact on the person who has asked you the question, you might also want to make eye contact from time to time with the other panel members.

2. If you don't understand a question, then in the first place you can ask for it to be repeated or clarified. If you still don't understand after the repetition/clarification, it is probably best to indicate this in your answer. For example, you could say something like: 'I am not sure if this is what you are looking for in the answer, but I think that the key points here are x, y and z.' If there is any possibility that you haven't properly understood the question, it is better to allude to this in your answer. Giving a completely off-the-wall

answer, without indicating to the panel that you know you may be way off-track, is potentially far more damaging to your chances.

3. It is to be hoped that the panel won't be giving you short, closed questions (except where they need to check out particular factual details, such as when you would be able to start in post). But if they do, resist the temptation to give one-word answers, and expand on the answer a little, regardless of the question.

4. If you don't know the answer to a factual question, don't ramble on in the hope of divine inspiration arriving mid-answer. In our experience, it tends not to be forthcoming! Instead, it is best to admit that you don't know the answer, smile, and explain that you have forgotten it, or that it is something you haven't experienced yet. If you can, offer an answer to a more generic situation related to the question, but that doesn't require you to remember a particular factual detail. (For example, if you are asked about the management of a particular condition in an elderly patient, and you have forgotten the details, or never knew them, we would suggest that you admit to your ignorance, and then say something about general approaches to care of the elderly.)

5. Long rambling answers are best avoided. As soon as you realise you have started to ramble, pause, gather your thoughts, provide a brief summary, and then finish off your answer.

6. Look through the suggested interview questions listed above and practise giving succinct answers. We would suggest that you say these answers out loud, rather than running through the points in your head. If you get into the habit of vocalizing your answer to the mirror, it can be less anxiety-provoking to hear yourself speaking in the actual interview. In addition, you can also practise not rushing through your answers, but using a slightly slower, clearer, rate of speech.

7. Think about your body language (not only eye contact, but also how you are sitting, whether you appear sufficiently, but not overly relaxed, etc.). If appropriate, a lightness of touch can go down well – but obviously this depends upon the situation. So, for example, if you are presented with a scenario involving a very distressing situation, we would not advise you to treat it in a light-hearted manner. But if you are asked about your weakness, you can (after first demonstrating insight through an appropriate discussion of a particular weakness) add a comment like: 'I also have a weakness for chocolate', or Manchester United, or whatever. But you have to use your professional judgement as to whether such comments would be appropriate

or not (just as you use your judgement with patients as to whether, at a particular moment, a light-hearted comment would ease the situation, or cause great offence).

When it's your turn to ask questions

At the end of the interview you may be asked if you have any questions. (If your interview is only 10–15 minutes, this might not happen.)

If they do ask you for your questions, avoid putting a question for the sake of it. Interviews are tiring for the panel, as well as for the candidates, and interviewers don't appreciate being asked pointless questions.

If you really haven't got a sensible question, say something like: 'All the questions that I had planned to ask have been covered in your explanation of the post. 'This means that you don't end the interview by responding with a curt 'No'.

However, it is a good idea to have a couple of suitable questions up your sleeve. Possibilities include the following:

1. What impact do you think the MMC reforms will have on the training in this deanery?
2. Are there any opportunities, at a later date, for sub-specialty training in x, y, or z? (But make sure that the answer to this question is not covered in any readily available information about the training programme.)
3. What have the trainees who have just finished training in x specialty in this hospital gone on to do?

Presentations

Prior to the MMC reforms, interviews for entry into a specialist training programme, or for consultant posts, typically involved you giving a presentation. At present you would probably not be expected to give a presentation during an interview for entry on to a foundation programme. However, you may be asked to give a presentation during an interview for a basic specialty training programme. And starting in 2008, some specialties required the applicant to devise the presentation on the day of the interview – i.e. they did not supply the title of the presentation in advance. We have included guidelines for preparing a presentation to be given as part of an interview in Appendix D.

Selection centres

One of the recommendations of the Tooke Inquiry into MMC was for the need to develop more robust selection systems.

A number of specialties are now using 'selection centres' as part of the recruitment and selection process. This approach is based on the idea that you end up with more robust selection decisions if you present applicants with tasks that reflect the actual activities that they would have to carry out in the job to which they are applying. So for example, the selection centre that is used in General Practice includes 3 exercises: an encounter with a simulated patient; a group exercise and a written exercise. These activities are observed and assessed by trained assessors.

If the specialty to which you are applying is using a selection centre approach, you will be provided with information about the selection centre as part of the information available for applicants. There is often little specific preparation that you can do for the selection centres above making yourself familiar with the person specification of the post for which you are applying. However, you may find it helpful to look at a DVD produced by the Association of Graduate Careers Advisory Services entitled 'Selection Centres for Specialty Training'. Ask the Centre Manager in your postgraduate education centre, or the careers specialists at your deanery for further information.

Final comments

In writing this chapter, we feel as if we have left you on something of a cliff-hanger. We have given detailed guidance on decision making and plan implementation – and after that you can't progress your plans any further until you have heard the results of the selection process.

If you are successful, we hope that the structured advice given in this handbook has helped you to make a robust career decision, and that you are looking forward to getting going with the next stage of your career.

If you are unsuccessful, you might be in a very different state of mind. In our experience (both personal, and also from our client work), we know how demoralised and hurt people can feel when they have put a huge amount of work into an application process which ultimately ends up in rejection. It's often a very depressing position to be in.

But, in time, you will have to pick yourself up, dust yourself down, and work out your next steps.

The first thing to do is to try to get as much information as possible about your unsuccessful application, because the more information you have, the better position you are in to review your next step.

After this, we would advise you to go through a brief review of the career-planning framework, to see if you want to change your choices or not. If you decide not to, you will then need to concentrate on Stage 4, to see how you can increase your chances of a subsequent application being successful.

We would also like to add two further observations.

The first is that a myth has been circulating in medical recruitment that for each doctor there is really only one career option that would suit them. In part, we think that this is a by-product of the old days when, at interviews for higher specialist training, you had to demonstrate your undying devotion to that specialty, and no other.

But this myth doesn't have psychological validity. Instead, as we described in Chapter 2, the psychological literature suggests that each doctor could be well suited to a number of different specialties (although there would definitely be others that would not suit them well). So we would encourage you to be flexible in your thinking – in particular about the 'O' in the ROADS acronym, i.e. 'opportunities'. Go back and see if there are other options that you hadn't considered previously which might suit you well.

The second observation relates to the first, and is that even within specialties there is enormous variation in the day-to-day details of what people actually do. For example, a GP in a single-handed rural practice and a GP in a large multi-partner health-centre practice will have some duties in common, but other aspects of their daily work will differ enormously.

What this means is that even when you have successfully navigated yourself through the maze of specialty training, the demands of career decision making are not over. Quite the contrary in fact, as you will have to make important career decisions throughout your professional life, up to and including the time you decide to retire. (Examples include whether you want to do sub-specialty training, become a GP with a Special Interest, developing teaching or management responsibilities, flexible or part-time working, etc.)

The four-stage model outlined in this handbook has been targeted at medical students and junior doctors. But it can actually be adapted to guide you through any career decisions that you will face in the future. It needs one further addition though (and for this we are grateful to Fiona McNamara from the University of Edinburgh careers service), and this is the addition of an 'R' for review.

Figure 5: Four-stage career-planning model plus review

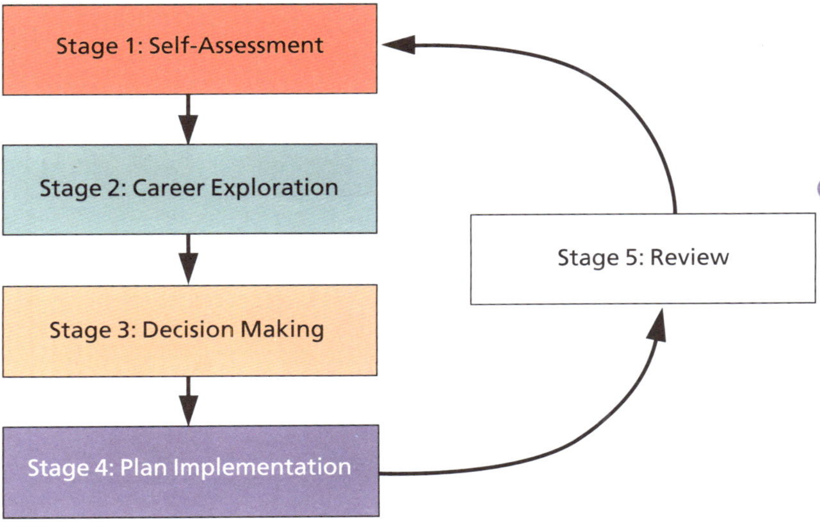

In effect, the four-stage model should become a circular, reflective cycle, rather than a static framework with a beginning and an end. And, as such, we hope that you will find it useful throughout the whole of your professional career.

Make Cakes Not War. Scribe Publications

GUIDELINES FOR THE EDUCATIONAL SUPERVISOR VI

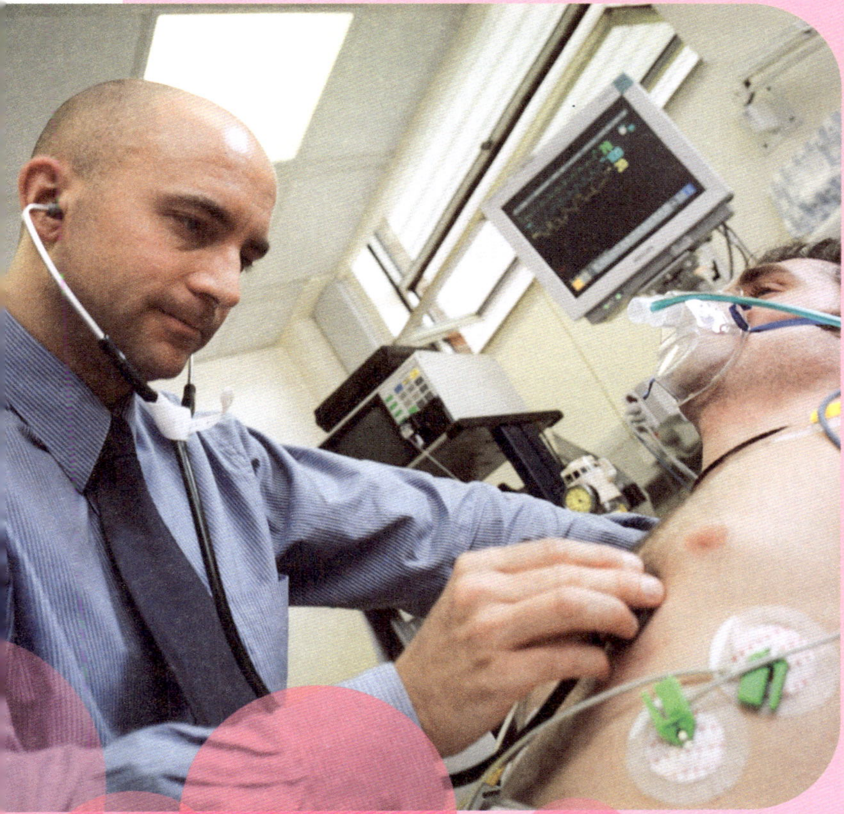

VI. GUIDELINES FOR THE EDUCATIONAL SUPERVISOR

Overview

This chapter begins with a brief description of the key players in postgraduate career support at trust level (namely Clinical Tutor/Director of Medical Education, the Foundation Programme Training Director and, in some deaneries, the Faculty Careers Lead). It then moves on to describing both the broader and career support responsibilities of the educational supervisor, and looks in detail at the specific concerns that consultants often express about the career support aspects of their educational supervisory role. Specific guidelines are given about supporting trainees whose career plans you believe to be unrealistic as well as supporting trainees who are contemplating leaving medicine.

The chapter then provides guidance on how to approach a 1:1 career-planning discussion with your trainee, and gives examples of the sorts of issues you might discuss in each of the four career planning stages. Although the emphasis of the chapter is on the provision of 1:1 support, the chapter ends with guidance on running group career-planning workshops. Detailed suggested teaching plans for these workshops are included in Appendices E and F.

Key players in the delivery of career support

It can be helpful to think about tiers of career support.

The first tier of support will typically be provided by educational supervisors as they are most likely to be able to take a more informed and constructive role about a particular trainee's strengths and weaknesses.

The second tier of support is typically provided by the trust Directors of Postgraduate Medical Education (DMEs), which is the new term for trust Clinical Tutors. Sitting alongside the DMEs, the Foundation Programme Training Directors and, if your deanery has them, the Faculty Careers Leads can also be called upon to provide second-tier support.

The third tier of support is that provided by the deanery-based careers team. Typical referrals to this team include a trainee who is struggling to make decisions, someone who is hanging on to plans which all concerned feel are desperately unrealistic, or a trainee who is seriously considering leaving medicine. In addition, senior clinicians within the Foundation School sometimes call upon the deanery careers team when a particular trainee is causing concern and seems to be finding it hard to settle into their role.

Ideally, everybody who provides career support should be appropriately trained for the level of support that they provide. Within many deaneries, basic training has been provided for educational supervisors on how best to support trainees with their career planning. For the second tier, the National Association of Clinical Tutors (NACT) provides relevant training (and currently it is being delivered by one of the authors of this book). As for the third tier, these are people like us who are qualified careers professionals, so the task there is continuing professional development rather than basic skills training. Organisations such as AGCAS (Association of Graduate Careers Advisory Services) provide professional training that is highly relevant to staff offering third-tier support.

Defining 'you'

The previous five chapters were written for the foundation trainee or medical student. In contrast, this chapter is written with the educational supervisor in mind. (In effect the 'you' that we have in mind when writing this handbook has switched. Throughout Chapters 1–5, the 'you' has represented the recipient of career support, while in this chapter the 'you' becomes the educational supervisor.)

Shared framework

We want to return briefly to the first chapter, where reference was made to a study by Hirsh et al (2001). In this study it was found that in workplace career discussions, if *both* participants had a common framework the recipients found the career discussions more productive. Bearing this finding in mind, it should be clear that you (the educational supervisor) should read through and 'digest' the contents of the first five chapters. (And, in fact, you might also want to try out some of the exercises yourself, as that way you will be in a better position to discuss them with your trainees.)

The role of the educational supervisor

The Guide to Postgraduate Specialty Training in the UK (The Gold Guide) published in 2007 by the four UK Health Departments outlines the roles of educational and clinical supervisor. It is clear from this guide that the same person may provide clinical and educational supervision, although it is also acceptable if the roles are split, as long as there is appropriate liaison between the two supervisors.

Digressing for a brief moment, it is necessary to refer to some educational theory, in order to clarify the differences in roles.

If you look at a standard textbook on the theory of assessment (e.g. Freeman and Lewis, 1998), you will find explanations about the difference between formative and summative assessment.

Formative assessment aims to provide feedback to the trainee, so that they are in a position to be able to improve their work. It tends to be provided during a period of training, rather than simply at the end. Formative assessment attempts to uncover both the strengths and weaknesses in a trainee's work.

In contrast, summative assessment counts towards or constitutes a final assessment or qualification. It involves making a professional judgement about the adequacy (or otherwise) of different aspects of the trainee's work.

Applying these terms to the context of foundation training, within the operational framework, both educational and clinical supervisors have to be trained to carry out competence assessments of foundation trainees (i.e. summative assessment). In addition, educational supervisors have to provide educational appraisals (i.e. formative assessments), to enable the trainee to reflect on their learning, and then jointly agree on appropriate educational goals.

It is also the task of the educational supervisor to have regular discussions with their foundation trainees about their career plans, and refer them to second- (or even third-) tier support if necessary.

Educational supervisor as provider of career support

Having run training workshops for consultants in a number of deaneries, we know that consultants often express concern about the following issues:

1. Their level of expertise across the whole span of medical careers.
2. Can they provide high-quality advice?
3. The trainee with unrealistic career plans.
4. The trainee who is considering leaving medicine.

Each of these will be considered in turn.

You're not an expert across the whole range of medical careers

On courses when consultants say that they are worried about giving careers advice because they don't have sufficient information about all the different options available, we often draw parallels with our own career-counselling practices. Currently in our own private practices we are working with individuals in publishing, medicine, the wine trade, health policy research, journalism, financial services, veterinary medicine, telecommunications and production engineering. And while we know quite a lot about some of these fields, we might know relatively little about other occupations on the list.

But our role is not to be an 'expert' in each and every possible occupation (there are too many of them to achieve this). Instead, we need to know where our clients can find more information – printed and web-based, and also know how they can gain access to people who do have expertise in the field of interest.

Using the suggestions outlined in Chapter 3, you should be in a better position to direct trainees to appropriate resources, so that they can begin to access the information that they need in order to decide whether that particular option might suit them. Bear in mind, too, that if the trainee has worked their way through the Stage 1 exercises, they should be in a better position to know the sort of information that they want to find out about when they begin to explore particular options.

Concerns about the quality of careers advice

What about the concern that you might inadvertently give a trainee poor careers advice? We understand that this is a definite area of concern and we also know that you – the educational supervisors – are in front-line positions, in terms of receiving anxious and overwrought requests for help from your foundation trainees. In reality, making decisions is hard enough at the best of times, and in the current climate of uncertainty it is considerably harder.

In fact, currently it is almost impossible to give 'advice' as there are so many unknowns in the new system. However, we would suggest that advice giving is not your key role – even if the situation was much more stable. Instead, your role is to provide a 'route map' for the trainee through the rough terrain of career decision making, but it is up to the trainee to pick the final destination. Or to phrase it rather differently, your role is to ask challenging, insightful questions – but not to provide the answers.

On courses when we introduce this idea of providing a 'route map', but not the final destination, we are frequently challenged by consultants, who tell us that it is unrealistic. However, having had many heated discussions with consultants, over a number of years, we feel that much of the disagreement comes from an understandable confusion between two different aspects of the educational supervisory role, namely that of assessor (if you are carrying out a summative, competence assessment) and careers adviser (when you have a formative developmental discussion about the trainee's career plans).

Imagine the following scenario. In your role as clinical supervisor you have graded a particular trainee as 'borderline for F1 completion' on some of the assessment tools. In particular, their performance seems highly variable on some DOPS (Direct Observation of Procedural Skills) assessments.

But you are also an educational supervisor to this trainee, and during their educational appraisal they tell you that they want to apply for basic specialist training in surgery, with a long-term goal of training in a particularly competitive surgical specialty. What should you do?

First, if you are both educational and clinical supervisor to a particular trainee, when you are sitting down to have an appraisal meeting, you need to think about what hat you are wearing. In terms of your role as a summative assessor, you cannot (and must not) alter your professional judgement that your trainee has been 'borderline' on these competencies, just because they have set their heart on a career in surgery. But in terms of your role as a careers adviser, rather than agonising whether you should advise the trainee to reconsider their career choices, you should focus on asking the following sorts of challenging questions.

What does the trainee see as their key strengths?

How does this self-assessment of their key strengths fit in with some of the assessment evidence in their learning portfolio?

In which areas have they been assessed as being less strong? Are any of these areas important in terms of demonstrating suitability for surgical training?

Is there a match between their areas of personal weakness and areas which are critically important in terms of suitability for surgical training?

Have they researched the likely competitiveness for Basic Surgical Training?

What are their thoughts on the fact that competition for entry into Basic Surgical Training is going to be very tough, but they have not scored highly on the relevant key competencies?

Have they thought through the robustness of their decision using the ROADS criteria?

And we could go on and on …

Typically consultants then challenge us and say why not 'call a spade a spade', and just tell them that they are not suited for further training in surgery? We would argue that the challenging questions approach outlined above is more robust, for the following reasons.

1. The directive approach (i.e. 'If I were you, I'd ditch surgery') absolves the trainee from taking responsibility for their own decision making.

2. Posing challenging questions rather than providing answers makes it more likely that the discussion will be opened up, and the trainee will start to think critically about their position.

3. If you go down the 'If I were you' route, it is tempting for your own pet likes and dislikes to influence the advice you give. This means that you might be more likely to encourage the trainee to reconsider specialties of interest to you, and to avoid those you particularly disliked at medical school. But of course, the 'If I were you' route has a basic flaw: the trainee is not you.

4. Your opinion could possibly be wrong. (For example, perhaps something is going on in the trainee's private life that means that they have been sleeping poorly, and in turn getting poor assessment results. But the trainee knows that at medical school they received highly favourable feedback on their potential for surgical training.)

We want to reiterate that in suggesting you avoid the 'If I were you' advice-giving approach, we are not advocating that you avoid challenging the trainee's career decision making. But we are suggesting that you encourage the trainee to reflect on the robustness of their career plans by posing challenging questions, rather than pointing out the answers. And if you go down this route, any concern about providing poor advice should be much less acute.

In fact, what you should be concerned about is posing questions that are insufficiently challenging.

The trainee with unrealistic career plans

The lengthy example discussed above is obviously also relevant to the issue of the 'unrealistic' trainee. But it might also be helpful to mention a couple of other points.

First, if you are faced with a trainee who persists in wanting to pursue a career plan that you feel is completely unrealistic, we would suggest that you ask the trainee to go and discuss their plans with another colleague who is in that particular specialty, or with somebody (either a clinician or a careers adviser) who has had additional training in career support. You should then do a brief summary outlining your own concerns about the robustness of their career plans and give it to the person who will be providing this additional support.

Secondly, on courses, we often end up discussing the difference between behaving responsibly 'to' but not being responsible 'for' the trainee. As outlined above, we would suggest that part of being responsible 'to' the trainee involves the provision of clear, constructive feedback about how they are performing in their current role; encouraging the trainee to carry out stages 1–3 of the career-planning process and challenging the robustness of proposed career plans using the ROADS criteria. All of these are ways in which you are behaving responsibly 'to' the trainee.

But you are not responsible 'for' the trainee.

If your trainee wants to ignore clear feedback that you have given them about their below-average performance in the current job, or ignore the facts on how competitive it is to succeed in their chosen pathway, or ignore the fact that they can't really give a clear and coherent reason as to why they feel that they are suited to the specialty, then, ultimately, that is the trainee's decision.

This distinction might help you feel less anxious if a trainee insists on following what you feel is an ill-advised career pathway. Because if you have behaved responsibly 'to' the trainee, that is all that is required of you, and it is not always possible to stop some people from making poor career decisions.

The trainee who is contemplating leaving medicine

Trainees may consider leaving medicine for a variety of reasons. For some, the notion that they might not be suited to the profession had already started during their undergraduate training, while for others it is the demands of being a junior doctor, rather than a medical student, that make them want to reconsider their plans. And yet others might be influenced by feeling unsupported in a particular placement.

In addition, while some trainees who are considering leaving the profession experience difficulties with their training, and are perhaps regarded by their educational supervisors as possibly not being up to the job, others may be highly regarded by their supervisors.

Working through the structured approach to career planning outlined in this handbook, should help the trainee start to become clearer about their career plans. And if it seems that a lack of support in a current placement is contributing to their dissatisfaction with the profession, you would need to liaise with the Foundation Programme Training Director in your trust.

However, as both of us are providing individual career counselling to trainees who are considering leaving medicine, we know from experience that many of these trainees greatly value specialised career support. We would therefore suggest that if a trainee comes to you saying that they might want to leave the profession you begin by using the approach outlined below in this chapter, to see if it is a temporary issue that can be resolved relatively simply, or an issue relating to specific difficulties in a particular placement. But if, after further discussion, it seems that they are seriously considering leaving medicine, we would suggest that they access the additional third-tier career support or invest in some private career counselling.

Currently, given the flurry of activity around medical career counselling, a number of organisations are being set up to offer services. Just as with other sorts of counselling or psychotherapy, we would strongly recommend that your trainee checks that the practitioner is adequately accredited by a suitable professional organisation. A list of appropriate professional bodies is included in Appendix A.

We would also like to add one further observation. In our experience, consultants often feel a sense of personal failure when a trainee (particularly a good one) admits that they are considering leaving the profession. We would certainly want you, in your role as educational supervisor, to behave responsibly 'to' your trainee, in all the ways detailed above. Thus if they come to you saying that they are unhappy and might want to leave medicine, we would want you to provide a supportive, structured response, in order to see if it is a temporary problem that could be remedied in some way.

But if, after you provide this sort of response, the trainee still persists in wanting to leave medicine, then you are not responsible 'for' this decision, and it does not represent a personal failing on your part.

What we often point out when this issue is raised in training workshops is that if selection into medical school was a completely foolproof business, and if people did not change during their five years of undergraduate training, you would be right to feel that the trainee had, in some crucial way, been let down by the system. But of course selection into medical school is not completely foolproof, and people change during their undergraduate training. So for both of these reasons some trainees may correctly conclude that they don't want to stay in medicine.

Your responsibility is to ensure that they have thought through the decision adequately, and where appropriate received specialised career support. But you shouldn't automatically regard the exiting trainee as a personal failure.

How to approach a 1:1 career planning session with your trainee

One of the responsibilities of the educational supervisor is to have regular feedback meetings with your trainee. This means that you should devote some time to discussing your trainee's career plans at each educational appraisal meeting. However, depending upon how each particular trainee is furthering their career plans, you might want to concentrate on career issues during one session or even arrange a separate time when you specifically focus on their career plans.

At all costs, what you want to avoid is the trainee failing to engage with the necessity of identifying their next career move – and then going into panic mode at the beginning of the second foundation year, when recruitment for specialty training looms.

Use the four-stage approach

It was argued above that your central role, in terms of supporting career planning, is to provide your trainee with a 'route map' through the career-planning stages. So in your first session with your FY1 trainee we would suggest that you check their understanding of the overall four-stage career-planning framework, and then concentrate on Stages 1 and 2.

We cannot emphasise enough that good career decision making rests on the foundations of adequate self-assessment and career exploration. It is therefore imperative that you encourage your trainees to spend adequate time on these first two stages.

In subsequent sections, ways of supporting your trainee through each of the four career planning stages are described.

Ask your trainees to bring their learning portfolios and their career-planning folder to all of their meetings. This will help them to review their work, and also help them develop a systematic approach to their career planning.

We would also like to emphasise the importance of listening carefully to your trainee in these 1:1 meetings. (And a favourite adage that we often use on training courses is given that we have been equipped with two ears and one mouth, we should use them in those proportions.) One helpful way of monitoring whether you are listening with enough care is to try to monitor who is doing most of the talking. There might be times in a 1:1 educational appraisal meeting when you (the consultant) should do most of the talking. But in general, in career-planning sessions, you should be asking the questions, and contributing your feedback, while the trainee should be doing most of the talking.

In terms of helping the trainee reflect on their developing career plans, in the sections below we outline the sorts of questions that you should be posing to your trainees. But it is important to remember the parallel with clinical consultations described at the beginning of chapter 2: just as it is pointless worrying about the details of a treatment regimen until you have taken a clinical history, examined the patient, and at least formed a preliminary diagnosis, so too do you have to ensure that the earlier stages of career planning are in place before you start doling out advice on how to succeed at the application process.

Your trainee might also find it helpful if you agree on specific career-planning tasks that they will carry out between the 1:1 meetings, together with appropriate time-scales for their completion.

Weaving in your feedback

In your role of guiding your trainee through a structured framework of career planning, you also have a vital role in terms of providing them with feedback on their performance to date.

Using the learning portfolio (and any other relevant data), you need to weave in your own understanding of how they have been progressing. If this understanding accords with their self-assessment or developing career plans, then you need to say so. Equally, when there is a discrepancy between what they are saying about themselves and your own opinion – then you need (as described above) to highlight these discrepancies, in order to discuss them as fully as possible.

While we are advocating that you should encourage your trainee to engage in rigorous self-assessment, we are not advocating that this should take place in a vacuum. Instead, it is your task to use your understanding of this trainee's performance to confirm, or to pose constructive challenges to, what the trainee is saying about their career plans.

A summary of the key points for a 1:1 meeting with your trainee is included in Table 3.

Table 3: Summary of key points for a 1:1 meeting

- Spend some time discussing your trainee's career plans at each educational appraisal meeting and if necessary arrange an extra meeting devoted to career planning.
- Encourage your trainee not to leave career planning to the last minute.
- In your first session, review the overall four-stage career-planning model.
- Ask your trainee to bring their learning portfolio and their career-planning folder to all 1:1 meetings.
- Listening is key. Remember! We have two ears and one mouth – to be used in that proportion.
- Help your trainee to lay the groundwork by spending sufficient time on Stages 1 and 2.

- At the end of each meeting, ask your trainee to specify which career-planning tasks they will carry out, and within which specified time-scale.
- Ensure you provide them with clear, constructive feedback on their performance to date.
- Encourage them to use the learning portfolio (and any other relevant data) to enhance their understanding of how they have been progressing.
- If you are concerned that the trainee is being unrealistic, focus on challenging questions rather than directive advice.
- If necessary suggest that they talk through their career plans with a colleague. Before this meeting, provide your colleague with a brief report that outlines your concerns.

Helping your trainee with their self-assessments (Stage 1)

Your task here is to encourage the trainee to conduct a thorough self-assessment of their work values, skills and interests, as well as possibly completing a psychometric test of interests or personality. You also want to help the trainee to reflect on the results of these self-assessments, so that they are able to identify the implications of these exercises for their future career choices.

We would not, however, recommend that the trainee completes these exercises during the 1:1 meeting. Instead, we would suggest that the trainee should complete the exercises in their own time (or in a career-planning workshop), and that they should bring the completed exercises to the 1:1 session for further discussion.

In the table below (see Table 4), we give suggestions for the sorts of questions that you could helpfully pose to your trainee about the Stage 1 exercises. (These are only suggested questions, so called 'Starters for 10'. We are not advocating that you plough through the questions in Table 3 like a semi-structured psychiatric interview, but, rather, that you use the questions below to get a feel for how you can help your trainee become clearer about their core values, interests, skills, etc.)

Table 4: Good questions to pose to your trainee about the Stage 1 exercises

Work values

1. What do you see as your core work values?
2. What are the possible implications of any of your core work values for the career decisions that you are currently facing?
3. Thinking back to a time when you particularly enjoyed your work, what links can you see between the reasons for this enjoyment and your core work values?
4. What about the opposite, i.e. what links can you see between a time when you were particularly unhappy at work and your core work values?
5. How might your core work values change over time, and how might you adjust your career plans in order that there is an appropriate match for these anticipated changes in work values?

Achievements/skills/interests

1. Using the results from the exercise where you examined specific achievements, what key skills did you identify? Of these, which are you particularly interested in using at work?
2. Are there any key skills that you aren't using at work that you would like to be able to use, in order to find work more satisfying?
3. What key skills did you identify in your non-work example? Are there any there that you would be interested in using in a work context?
4. What factors contribute to you feeling stressed at work?

Psychometric instruments

1. (Before.) What are you hoping to gain from taking this particular instrument?
2. (After.) What are your thoughts about the results? To what extent do the results accord with what you already know about yourself? Can you give specific examples? And to what extent do the results conflict with what you already know about yourself? (And again, can you give specific examples?)

Summary of Stage 1

1. If you were asked to give a summary of the self-assessment exercises that you carried out as part of Stage 1, what would you say?
2. Can you think of examples from your career to date that illustrate the individual pattern of values, skills, interests, etc. that you have included in your summary?
3. If you do not feel at all clear about your key values, skills, interests, etc., what are you going to do in order to enhance your ability to complete the Stage 1 exercises in sufficient detail?

Helping your trainee explore different career options (Stage 2)

The key task for you in this stage is to encourage your trainee to conduct a systematic exploration of different career options that interest them. Furthermore, as has been argued throughout, this career exploration does not involve researching each option in a standardised way, but, instead, you need to encourage your trainee to construct a personalised list of queries (derived from the Stage 1 self-assessments) and then apply this personalised list to the specific careers that they are exploring further.

All the points discussed in the sections above (e.g. good listening combined with asking challenging questions) also apply to how you should support your trainee through their Stage 2 activities.

Good questions to pose to your trainee in this stage of the career planning framework are included in Table 5 *(overleaf)*.

Table 5: Good questions to pose to your trainee about the Stage 2 exercises

1. Have you identified two to four options that you want to explore further? If yes, then go to question 3, if no, then go to question 2.
2. What specific tasks are you going to carry out in order to be able to identify a suitable short-list of possible options? (This might include going back to redo the Stage 1 exercises in more detail, arranging to complete a psychometric instrument such as Sci59 or the Myers-Briggs Type Indicator. Or it might involve getting some additional 1:1 support such as arranging a session with the Faculty Careers Lead or the Senior Careers Adviser in your deanery.)
3. (If the educational supervisor has concerns about any of the choices being explored.) On the basis of what I have seen of your work/your assessments, it seems as if (name the relevant competence) is something that you struggle with. Yet this would be a key aspect of training in (name the specialty). How do you reconcile these two facts?
4. Having identified two to four options that you want to explore further, have you constructed a list of specific questions (linked to the Stage 1 self-assessment activities) that you are going to explore? Having done this, for each question, have you worked out what you are going to read/whom you are going to ask? What time-scale have you set yourself?
5. Have you identified a 'back-up plan' in case you are not successful in achieving your first-choice option? If not, do you think that this might be a useful strategy? How might you go about choosing your 'back-up plan'?

Helping your trainee make a good career decision (Stage 3)

Your key task here is to help your trainee make a final decision as to what they are going to apply for on their application form. You should also help them interrogate the robustness of this decision using the ROADS criteria.

Good questions to pose to your trainee in this stage of the career-planning framework are included in Table 6.

Table 6: Good questions to pose to your trainee about Stage 3

1. Looking back at the Lifeline exercise, can you identify a good career decision that you have made in the past? With reference to this example, how did you arrive at this decision?
2. What can you learn from this previous decision in terms of how best to approach your current decision?
3. How would you explain your career decision in terms of the match between what you now understand about yourself (Stage 1) and what you have found out about the career options that you wish to pursue (Stage 2)?
4. Have you reviewed your decision using the ROADS checklist? **Realistic** – are you being realistic about yourself AND the demands of the job? **Opportunities** – have you given serious consideration to all the opportunities available? **Anchors** – have you built in the things that provide support in your life? **Development** – do your choices fully develop your potential? **Stress** – have you considered those aspects of work that pose particular stresses for you?
5. Have you identified both a plan, and a 'back-up plan'? (If, as the educational supervisor, you think that the plan and/or the 'back-up' fail to meet one or more of the ROADS criteria, then you need to raise this issue with your trainee. If your trainee doesn't want to take the questions that you are challenging them with on board, then you can suggest that they go and discuss their career plans with the Faculty Careers Lead or the Deanery Careers Adviser.)

Helping your trainee with implementing their plans (Stage 4)

At this stage you need to discuss the application forms with your trainee, and also ensure that they are doing adequate interview preparation.

Application forms

The issue of how far it is permissible to help your trainees with their application forms is a vexed one. If you are going to be involved in short-listing or interviewing, then it is probably advisable if you suggest that your trainee has a more detailed conversation about their application form or about the interview with another colleague.

We would suggest that you encourage the trainees to read through the detailed advice given in the relevant sections of this handbook. In addition (as long as you are not actually involved in the short-listing or interview process), you can read through drafts of their answers and make *general* comments. For example, it is permissible to make general comments such as: 'I don't think that you have adequately answered the second part of the question' or 'I don't think that your answer clearly demonstrates that you have all the necessary skills.' You should, however, avoid suggesting specific wording that they should include in the form.

The sorts of questions that you could pose to your trainee at this stage of the career-planning process are included in Table 7.

Table 7: Good questions to pose to your trainee about application forms

1. Have you carefully read through Chapter 3 in this handbook?
2. Are you clear that you are going to meet the application deadlines?
3. Have you checked that your answers tally with the specific criteria as outlined in the person specification? (But, equally, have you made sure that your answers do not involve simply repeating the wording of the person specification on your actual application form?)
4. Have you checked and re-checked your spelling and grammar?

Interviews

Using the sample interview questions included in Chapter 3, you can conduct mock interviews with your trainees. You can either do this on a 1:1 basis, or can incorporate interview training into a group career-planning workshop (see below). But, again, we would suggest that you don't run a mock interview for a trainee (or group of trainees) if you are actually on the interviewing panel.

In terms of discussing interview preparation during a 1:1 session with your trainee, the sorts of questions that you might want to ask are included in Table 8.

Table 8: Good questions to pose to your trainee about interviews

1. Have you thought about the questions that you are highly likely to be asked, and planned some strong answers? (You can then discuss these.)
2. Have you prepared a small number of examples (taken from your learning portfolio) that clearly demonstrate your key skills and abilities? Have you also prepared some suitable examples in case you are asked about areas in which you are weaker, or about mistakes that you have made in the past? (And, again, you can discuss these.)
3. What specific concerns do you have about the interview process? How are you intending to address these concerns? Who else could help you?

Group career-planning workshops

In some regions career-planning workshops have been incorporated into the generic taught foundation programme.

This is a strategy that we would advocate; not only is it an efficient use of time, but also the trainees can learn much, and gain encouragement and support from each other.

The person running the workshop doesn't need to be a 'careers expert', as all the necessary basic materials have been worked out for you, and are detailed below. Instead, the role of the person running the workshop is to act as a facilitator.

Many of the basic guidelines described above about how best to approach the task of 1:1 careers meetings also apply to the task of group facilitation. For example, as with a 1:1 meeting, in a group session it is also important to:

1. Outline the overall four-stage career planning framework.
2. Listen carefully to the points that the trainees are making.
3. Pose challenging questions.

But there are a few points that apply specifically to the group situation. Specifically, we would highlight the following:

Avoid the discussion of highly personal issues (such as whether in future they might want to have a family) in front of the group. This can be discussed by setting a task for the whole group, getting the group to discuss it in smaller groups, and then reconvening when you ask for *general* comments. Trainees are much more likely to speak openly to small groups of their peers than in larger groups, in which the consultant is present.

If you are asking them to reflect on negative issues (what they find stressful, mistakes, etc.), get them to discuss this in pairs, or perhaps to write down their thoughts on their own. You shouldn't ask the trainees to discuss what could be quite painful issues in a small- or large-group context. For these tasks use paired work, or ask them to work individually.

Provide time at the end of the session for trainees to come and speak to you in private. If the issue they raise turns out to be quite a complex one, you might need to arrange an additional time, or suggest a referral to another source. But, in our experience, at the end of sessions trainees often come and raise issues in private that they did not feel comfortable raising in front of the whole group.

One advantage of a group context is that they can learn from each other. So if a trainee asks you a challenging question, if appropriate pose it back to the group for comments, before you wade in with your own answer. Often the group will come up with excellent answers, and the trainees find the support and advice of their peers particularly helpful.

Final comments

Having run a large number of training workshops for consultants, we know that some educational supervisors feel distinctly uneasy about their career support responsibilities.

It is our hope that the structured four-stage model outlined in this chapter will provide you with a practical framework for approaching the task. The following figure provides an overview of the activities which need to be covered.

Figure 6: Foundation programme – overview of activities

	Foundation year 1		Foundation year 2	
Career-planning stage	**Trainee doctors**	**Foundation programme team**	**Trainee doctors**	**Foundation programme team**
Stage 1 – self-assessment	Interests Values Skills and achievements Stresses and strains Psychometric tests (optional)	Run workshop 1 for F1 doctors to introduce the career-planning framework and cover Stages 1 and 2 in greater detail – see Appendix E Educational supervisors to review career planning in 1:1 meetings with trainees	Review Stage 1 and 2 assessments in order to prepare for Stage 3	Educational supervisors to review career planning in 1:1 meetings with trainees
Stage 2 – career exploration	Initial search to identify possible career options More focused search, including interviewing people in the specialties of interest Attend events, including career fairs	Run workshop 1 as above Educational supervisors to review career planning in 1:1 meetings with trainees	The trainee considers their career options in light of any changes in their Stage 1/2 activities	Educational supervisors to review career planning in 1:1 meetings with trainees

Continued overleaf

	Foundation year 1		Foundation year 2	
Career-planning stage	**Trainee doctors**	**Foundation programme team**	**Trainee doctors**	**Foundation programme team**
Stage 3 – decision making	When ready, the trainee moves on to Stage 3		The trainee considers their career options Decision-making exercise ROADS	Run workshop 2 for F2 doctors to include a brief review of the career-planning framework and to cover Stages 3 and 4 – see Appendix F Educational supervisors to review career planning in 1:1 meetings with trainees
Stage 4 – plan implementation			Application forms Interviews	Run workshop 2 as above Educational supervisors to review career planning in 1:1 meetings with trainees

Chapter 2 began with a clinical analogy, namely comparing the four-stage career-planning framework to a model of clinical consultation, and we would like to return briefly to this parallel, in the final section of the handbook.

As experienced clinicians, your approach to a clinical consultation will by now be second nature to you, as it is something that you do without thinking, day in, day out. But the same isn't true for your medical students (and wasn't true for you when you were a medical student). This therefore reminds us that learning a complex new skill takes both time and practice.

Putting the framework outlined in this handbook into practice will take a bit of time to get used to, as there are both information to assimilate and skills to develop. And you will also need to practise it. But you are starting from a good vantage point given that you already have a highly developed set of communication skills that you use in your patient consultations (and also in teaching and management tasks).

Often at the end of workshops consultants express relief that a task that they had previously felt was beyond their expertise (namely the provision of career support) turned out to be much more straightforward than they had initially envisaged.

We hope that by using this handbook, you will reach a similar conclusion.

Copyright: Judy Horacek 2006. *Make Cakes Not War*. Scribe Publications

Bibliography

Ali, L. and Graham, B. (1996). *The Counselling Approach to Careers Guidance*. London: Taylor and Francis (Routledge)

Borges, N. J. and Savickas, M. L. (2002). 'Personality and medical specialty choice: a literature review and integration', *Journal of Career Assessment*, 10, no. 3, pp. 362–80

Borges, N. J., Savickas, M. L. and Jones, B. J. (2004). 'Holland's theory applied to medical specialty choice', *Journal of Career Assessment*, 12, no. 2, pp. 188–206

Cochran, L. (1997). *Career Counselling: a Narrative Approach*. London: Sage

Covey, S. (2004). *7 Habits of Highly Effective People*. London: Simon and Schuster

Freeman, R. and Lewis, R. (1998). *Planning and Implementing Assessment*. London: Kogan Page

Gale, R. and Grant, J. (2002). 'Sci45: the development of a specialty choice inventory', *Medical Education*, 36 (7), pp. 659–66

Gallwey, W. T. (2001). *The Inner Game of Work*. London: Random House

Hirsh, W., Jackson, C. and Kidd, J. M. (2001). *Straight Talking: Effective Career Discussions at Work*. Cambridge: National Institute for Careers Education and Counselling (NICEC)

Hopson, B. and Scally, M. (2000). *Build Your Own Rainbow: Workbook for Career and Life Management*. London: Kogan Page

Kapes, J. T., Mastie, M. M. and Whitfield, E. A. (eds.) (1994). *A Counsellor's Guide to Career Assessment Instruments*. 3rd edn. National Career Development Association

Kersley, S. (2005). *Prescription for Change*. Oxford: Radcliffe

Kersley, S. (2006). *ABC of Change for Doctors*. Oxford: Radcliffe

Kidd, J. M. (2006). *Understanding Career Counselling: Theory, Research and Practice*. London: Sage

Landsberg, M. (2003). *The Tao of Coaching*. London: Profile Books

Lepnurm, R., Danielson, D. and Dobson, R. (2006). 'Cornerstones of career satisfaction in medicine', *Canadian Journal of Psychiatry*, 51, no. 8, pp. 512–22

Nathan, R. and Hill, L. (2006). *Career Counselling*. 2nd edn. London: Sage

Reid, H. and Bimrose, J. (eds.) *Constructing the Future: Transforming Career Guidance*. Institute of Career Guidance

Schein, E. H. (1990). *Career Anchors: Discovering Your Real Values:* Instrument. USA: Jossey-Bass.Pfiefer

Tooke J. *Aspiring to excellence: final report of the independent inquiry into Modernising Medical Careers*. London: MMC Inquiry, 2008. www.mmcinquiry.org.uk

Ward, C. and Eccles, S. (2001). *So You Want to be a Brain Surgeon? Oxford:* Oxford University Press

Watts, A.G, Law, W., Killeen, J., Kidd, J. M. and Hawthorn, R. (1996). *Rethinking Careers Education and Guidance*. London: Routledge

Whitmore, J. (2002). *Coaching for Performance:* Growing People, Performance and Purpose. National Book Network

Yost, E. B. and Corbishley, M. A. (1987). *Career Counselling: a Psychological Approach*. USA: Jossey-Bass.Pfiefer

Appendix A
Career Counsellors: List of Professional Bodies

Within the career-counselling profession the words information, advice and guidance have specific meanings:

Information – this is the provision of information on learning and work which can be provided through a wide range of media like websites, leaflets, etc. and face to face. Within the medical education context information about specialty training opportunities, competition ratios, etc. are good examples.

Advice – this is where someone might wish to discuss the information they have gathered with someone to develop their understanding of it and find out if there are other sources of information which would be useful to them. The person giving the advice might propose they need more in-depth support and this is where guidance comes in.

Guidance – the provision of in-depth support to an individual, often face to face or by telephone. Increasingly, electronic media are being used to provide guidance and it's also often provided in a group setting.

Please note that career counsellors are also often called career advisers, career guidance professionals, career consultants and career practitioners. Increasingly, people are also offering career coaching.

Institute of Career Guidance: http://www.icg-uk.org/find.html
The ICG accredits career guidance professional and has a section on its website to help you find a career adviser.

AGCAS: http://www.agcas.org.uk/
The Association of Graduate Careers Advisory Services is the professional association of career professionals in Higher Education. University Careers Services are usually members of AGCAS and your medical school may have access to the services of the university careers service.

Prospects: http://www.prospects.ac.uk/cms/ShowPage/Home_page/p!eLaXi
This is the UK's official website for graduates and it is supported by AGCAS. You can email a careers consultant and also find a career coach if you want to work with someone on an individual basis. These services are included in the careers advice section of the website.

NAEGA: http://www.naega.org.uk/
The National Association for Educational Guidance for Adults is a practitioner organisation run by members for members. The website has links to guidance providers in its 'looking for guidance' section.

British Psychological Society: http://www.bps.org.uk/
The BPS is the representative body for psychology and psychologists in the UK. You can use their main site to find a chartered psychologist.
The BPS also accredits practitioners in the use of psychometric instruments and has a separate website for the Psychological Testing Centre: http://www.psychtesting.org.uk/. The directories section contains details of qualified testers, and within the directories section you need to search for a Level B instrument (as personality instruments such as the MBTI are categorised as Level B).

Coaching

Coaching is an increasingly popular tool which can be used to help support personal development. It can also be offered as life coaching, career coaching, personal development coaching, etc. The European Coaching Institute defines coaching as a 'simple yet effective form of personal development where client and coach create an alliance that promotes and sustains the client's personal growth and competence'.

At the moment there are no official regulatory standards for coaching and no governed training standards which need to be attained before individuals can become a coach. There are though two internationally self-appointed accreditation bodies that aim to self-regulate the industry and within the UK CIPD (Chartered Institute of Personnel and Development) provide advice to HR professionals on coaching and mentoring.

Here are some websites if you would like to find out more:

CIPD:
http://www.cipd.co.uk/subjects/lrnanddev/coachmntor/default.htm?IsSrchRes=1
European Coaching Institute: http://www.europeancoachinginstitute.org/
International Coach Federation: http://www.coachfederation.org/icf/

Appendix B
Further Resources for Career Planning

General career planning

Hopson, B. and Scally, M. (2000). *Build Your Own Rainbow:* Workbook for Career and Life Management. London: Kogan Page

(This can also be used as a self-help guide by trainees who want more help with Stage 1.)

Medical career guides

AGCAS DVD –Selection centres for speciality training. *http://www.agcas.org.uk/agcas_resources/37-selection-centres-for-speciality-training*

Chambers, R., Mohanna, K. and Field, S. (2000). *Opportunities and Options in Medical Careers*. Oxford: Radcliffe Medical Press

Cottrell, E., Rebora, C. and Williams, M. (2006). *The Medical Student Career Handbook.* Oxford: Radcliffe Publishing

Hastie, A. and Stephenson A. (2008). *Choosing General Practice*. Oxford: Blackwell Publishing

MacDonald, R. and Hadridge, P. (2003). *My Beautiful Career*. London: BMJ Publishing Group

Ward, C. and Eccles S. (2001). *So You Want to be a Brain Surgeon?* Oxford: Oxford University Press

(This book probably has the most detailed description of different career options for doctors. It was written before MMC was introduced though.)

Royal College of Physicians of London (2002). *Careers Information Handbook for Trainees.* London: Royal College of Physicians

Royal College websites

These sites contain a wide range of information including person specifications, information about education and training, flexible training, etc.

- Academy of Royal Colleges: http://www.aomrc.org.uk/
- College of Emergency Medicine: http://www.emergencymed.org.uk/cem/
- Royal College of Anaesthetists: http://www.rcoa.ac.uk/
- Faculty of Dental Surgery: http://www.rcseng.ac.uk/fds
- Royal College of General Practitioners: http://www.rcgp.org.uk/
- Royal College of Obstetricians and Gynaecology: http://www.rcog.org.uk/
- Faculty of Occupational Medicine: http://www.facoccmed.ac.uk/

- Royal College of Ophthalmologists: http://www.rcophth.ac.uk/
- Royal College of Paediatrics and Child Health: http://www.rcpch.ac.uk/
- Royal College of Pathologists: http://www.rcpath.org/
- Faculty of Pharmaceutical Medicine: http://www.fpm.org.uk/
- Royal College of Physicians of Edinburgh: http://www.rcpe.ac.uk/
- Royal College of Physicians of London: http://www.rcplondon.ac.uk/
- Royal College of Physicians and Surgeons of Glasgow: http://www.rcpsglasg.ac.uk/
- Royal College of Physicians of Ireland: http://www.rcpi.ie/Default.aspx
- Royal College of Psychiatrists: http://www.rcpsych.ac.uk/
- Faculty of Public Health: http://www.fphm.org.uk/
- Royal College of Radiologists: http://www.rcr.ac.uk/
- Royal College of Surgeons of Edinburgh: http://www.rcsed.ac.uk/site/0/default.aspx
- Royal College of Surgeons of England: http://www.rcseng.ac.uk/
- Royal College of Surgeons in Ireland: http://www.rcsi.ie/

Medical careers websites

- NHS careers: http://www.nhscareers.nhs.uk/home.html
- BMJ careers: http://careers.bmj.com/careers/welcome.html
- Doctors.net: http://www.doctors.net.uk/
- UK Foundation Programme: http://www.foundationprogramme.nhs.uk/pages/home

Websites which advertise medical jobs and training opportunities

- National recruitment office for GP training: http://www.gprecruitment.org.uk/
- NHS Jobs: http://www.jobs.nhs.uk/
- BMJ careers: http://careers.bmj.com/careers/welcome.html
- Health Service Journal: http://www.hsj.co.uk/
- Hospital Doctor: http://www.totaljobs.com/minisites/hospitaldoctor/jobsearch.asp

Essential websites

- COPMeD is the Conference on Postgraduate Medical Deans in the UK: http://www.copmed.org.uk/
- PMETB regulates postgraduate medical education: http://www.pmetb.org.uk/
- Department of Health: http://www.dh.gov.uk/Home/fs/en – can be used to obtain a copy of the 'Gold Guide', which regulates specialty training
- MMC: http://www.mmc.nhs.uk

- GMC: http://www.gmc-uk.org/ – for copies of *'Good Medical Practice'* and *'The New Doctor'*
- BMA: http://www.bma.org.uk/ap.nsf/content/home – and ensure you have a copy of the *BMA Junior Doctors Handbook*
- Disability Rights Commission: http://www.drc-gb.org/ – the Disability Discrimination Act (1995) introduced a number of important provisions for employees: the guaranteed interview scheme and requiring employers to make reasonable adjustments for people with disabilities. The Disability Rights Commission's website contains useful information and advice.

Please note that all the website information was correct at the time of writing.

Psychometric tests

Sci45/59. Specialty Choice Inventory.
Available from the Open University Centre for Education in Medicine
Tel. 01908 653776

Available for BMA members from the BMA website. Some deaneries have also purchased licences for this instrument. Ask the Centre Manager at your trust Education Centre, or the deanery careers staff.

Appendix C
Guidelines for CV Writing

Introduction

There is considerable variability in recommended layouts and we would suggest that you discuss this matter with your educational supervisor and your colleagues. But whatever layout you choose, you need to make sure that the CV matches the person specification of the post to which you are applying. To do otherwise can give the impression that you aren't really that keen on being offered the post.

The issue of including information that identifies your age is also tricky. From a legal point of view, you do not need to include such information, so not only your date of birth but also the dates at which you achieved different qualifications can be omitted. However, although recruiters cannot mark you down for omitting this information, they might find it surprising, as many people would expect to put the dates at which they passed particular exams on their CV. Again, we would suggest that you get local advice from your educational supervisor.

The headings below give one possible structure, and it is certainly a useful starting point for constructing your final CV.

Personal details

Your name, address, telephone number, and email address – these should be at the top of page one of your CV and could be shown in a header on subsequent pages.

Career plan

One sentence summarising your career aims, and how the job on offer will help you achieve them.

Personal information

Include your GMC number and type of registration. You do not need to include your date of birth, nationality, marital status or sex.

Professional qualifications (from the current time, back to medical school, i.e. include most recent first).
So if you have completed additional professional qualifications (e.g. MRCP Part 1), this should go first. Then list your medical school qualifications. For each qualification list:

– Title of qualification, class of degree (if relevant), awarding body and, if you choose to, the date.
– In addition, bullet-point prizes/distinctions at medical school. You may also include a bullet point on your elective year, as part of the description of your undergraduate training.

Education

Details of your school qualifications with name of school and grades and again, if you choose to, the date. (Again, most recent first.)

Professional expertise

Include job title, locations and dates. For current and previous posts, beyond listing job title, employing trust and dates, you can also include a couple of bullet points highlighting the key features of each job that demonstrate your suitability for the post on offer. If you are a more experienced applicant who has had a number of previous medical jobs, then you don't want to give too much detail on jobs that you did a considerable time ago, or on jobs in which you basically gained the same experience. The key point here is that you don't need to give the same amount of information on each and every job that you include in your CV; matching to the person specification is the important task.

Practical skills

Bullet-point specific procedures you are familiar with and where relevant indicate how many you have performed. For example, 'performed more than 20 chest aspirations'.

Additional courses

List ALS or other relevant course.

Research

List your publications, case reports and conference presentations (but be wary of writing 'in preparation' as this can irritate consultants, who know that such claims often don't amount to much).

Teaching and audit

Include a couple of examples, and make sure you briefly mention the outcome of any audit.

Other relevant skills

For example, you can mention foreign languages that you speak, and particular IT skills.

Interests

Bullet-point a couple of your interests that you can talk about at interview and that add value to your application.

References

Give at least two references. One of the referees should be your current or most recent educational supervisor. Include accurate contact details for those referees and remember to let your referee know that you have given their details as a referee as this avoids unnecessary delays.

If you want more detailed guidance on CV writing, the following two books are useful:

How to Get a Job in Medicine: Adam Poole. Elsevier Health Sciences. 2005

Sam McErin. *Writing a Winning CV: Effective Professional Development.* Edukom. 2004

Appendix D
Guidelines for Giving a Presentation at a Job Interview

For some specialties you may be asked to give a presentation as part of the selection process. Usually the subject is given to you in advance together with the maximum time you have to deliver it on the day.

When the topic is given to you in advance

1. Preparation

   Start your preparation by researching and gathering your thoughts on the subject matter of the presentation and what you could cover. Ask colleagues, friends and others for their views on what should be included. Do be aware that it might be appropriate to bring in higher-level contextual information, e.g. a new policy on treatment for that particular specialty.

   Once you have an idea of what you think you will cover, organise your material and start thinking about the best way to present it.

2. PowerPoint

   Most people use packages like PowerPoint and that is fine. Do keep your slides simple, with a clean layout and effective colour scheme. Busy slides with lots of detail are often difficult to read and flying bullet points and flashy effects can be very irritating to interviewers. Also ensure you are familiar with the content as this will help you deliver a more fluent presentation.

   Keep the layout of your slides clean and simple. Diagrams can be effective and help you to make your point. They should be drawn in such a way that it is clear how they should be read. Keep the number of bullet points on the slides to no more than five or six and each bullet should act as a prompt for you to explain the point further.

3. Back-up

   Technology does sometimes let you down so do take along paper copies of the material which you can distribute and refer to if the technology fails. This shows good planning, and that you don't fall to pieces when the going gets tough.

4. Beginnings

   The presentation is likely to be early in the interview process so make sure you introduce yourself and the subject matter to the panel before you start. Take a deep breath and try to enjoy the presentation.

5. Positioning

   During the presentation be aware of where you are standing and make sure you don't obstruct the panel's view of your slides. You will also need to maintain eye contact with the panel. The focus of your presentation is the panel – so look at them and not the computer or the slides on the wall. If you need prompts for your presentation, prepare a set of notes which you keep to hand and can refer to. In addition, fluency comes from being very familiar with the contents of the presentation.

   Avoid at all costs turning your back on the interviewers and reading the points from the slides, and don't pace up and down! It can make the interviewing panel nervous.

6. Timing

   You will be asked to keep your presentation within a particular time-frame. Make sure you can stick to this, as some panels might stop you when you come to time, even if you haven't finished what you wanted to say.

7. Practice

   It is essential to practise your presentation out loud to yourself, and then ideally to an audience. See if you can find a small willing audience of friends and family to help you. This will also help you check that it is within the time limits. Going through it in your head takes a lot less time than speaking it out loud and will give you a false impression of how long it will take you on the day. Also, do think about the way your voice tone and pace might be affected by nerves on the day. You may speak faster or slower so do bear that in mind when you are checking your timing.

   Taking a deep breath before you start helps get oxygen to your brain. If at any time during the presentation you feel you are running out of breath or getting carried away, finish your next point, pause, take a deep breath and start again.

8. Questions

   Once you have completed your presentation the interviewers are likely to ask you some questions about it. Do think in advance what they might ask and prepare some suitable answers. There is always a possibility that one of the interviewers will ask you something which is in an unfamiliar area. You can't prepare for this. Take a moment or two to compose yourself, smile and then try to give the best answer possible.

When the topic is given to you on the day

In this situation, you obviously cannot prepare your presentation in advance. The only constructive preparation that you can do is to talk with friends and colleagues to think through possible topics that you might be given. Are there any particularly hot controversies in your specialty of interest? If there are, you might want to think through a brief summary of your views on the issue. (And you should do this anyway as a way of preparing for the questions that you might be asked at interview.)

But beyond thinking about possible topics, the other preparation you can usefully do is to work out how many 'bullet points' you can discuss in the allocated time. (Typically you will know how long the presentation is prior to the interview, even if you don't know the precise topic.) So you might want to have a dummy run with a topic that you make up yourself – just to see how much content you can comfortably cover in the given time span.

If the topic is given to you on the day you will be provided with acetates and pens rather than being expected to do an 'on-the-spot' PowerPoint presentation. Make sure that your writing is clear, that you spell words correctly, and that you don't try to stuff too much content onto each acetate.

It is also important that you don't set yourself impossible standards. If they give you the topic on the day they are assessing how quickly you can construct a well ordered coverage of the topic – they are not expecting you to know every last fact, or have beautifully hand illustrated acetates. So try to keep calm, spend most of the preparation time on ordering your argument, and then in the actual presentation just include a few acetates with a small number of bullet points on each acetate.

Beyond this points 4, 5 and 7 listed above also apply. (In terms of 7. 'practice', you clearly can't practise the actual presentation, but you can practise giving a presentation with a topic of your own choice in order to get used to the sound of your voice, speaking at an appropriate pace and re-starting if you go blank during the time that you are speaking. As mentioned above, this practice can also help you work out how much content you can comfortably cover in the allocated time.

Appendix E

Workshop 1 – Introduction to career-planning seminar for F1 trainees

Introduction

This workshop has been designed to introduce career planning to foundation programme trainees and should be held early on in their F1 year. All trainees should be encouraged to attend and will need to bring along this resource book.

For this workshop you should ideally allocate at least two hours to ensure the material is covered adequately. The timings given below are for a workshop lasting two and a half hours.

- Purpose of the session and introduction: 15 minutes;
- Brief overview of the four stages: 10 minutes;
- Stage 1 self-assessment: 60 minutes;
- Short break: 15 minutes;
- Stage 2 career exploration: 30 minutes;
- Plenary: 20 minutes.

The timings can be amended to cover the material in a two- or three-hour session by either reducing the break and plenary session for a two-hour session or increasing the time spent on Stages 1 and 2 for a three-hour session.

Workshop plan

Time	Activity	Teaching notes	Resources
15 mins	Explain the purpose of the session and a brief introduction.	Explain the four stages: 1. Self-assessment: work values and skills and interests. 2. Career exploration: research into different career pathways. 3. Decision making. 4. Plan implementation. Introductory comments: a. The four-stage framework is one that applies to career decision making at any stage of one's career – it is not restricted to the current career decisions that the foundation trainees are facing. b. This introductory session won't provide the trainees with all the answers, i.e. they won't be 'sorted' by the end of the session. Instead, the session aims to provide trainees with a sense of the questions that they need to ask themselves over the coming weeks/months, plus ways of finding answers to these questions – so that by the Jan/Feb of their F2 year they are more likely to make a sound career decision. c. The session will concentrate on Stages 1 and 2, but will also touch on the other two stages in less detail. These other stages will be covered in more detail in subsequent sessions. d. This introductory session is still useful to those trainees who already feel that they have made their mind up about their post-foundation career. Why? First of all, it is useful to check if their career decision making is robust. Secondly, Stage 4 (plan implementation) depends on the previous stages. If the decision rests on a firm foundation of self-assessment (Stage 1), career exploration (Stage 2), and how these match together (Stage 3), the trainee will be better equipped to write a convincing application form and provide good answers at interview.	Trainees to have access to this book and bring their foundation portfolios.

Time	Activity	Teaching notes	Resources
	Stage 1 self-assessment	Run two Stage 1 exercises: work values and skills/achievements	Chapter II
30 mins	Stage 1 self-assessment	**Exercise 1: work values** Explain that work values have been found to be an important predictor of occupational satisfaction. Then explain how to do the card sort. After the trainees have sorted the cards (on their own), encourage them to pair up and talk through the questions. Reconvene as a group, and ask the trainees for any comments. You might also ask them to think about times at work when they have been particularly satisfied (or, for that matter, particularly dissatisfied), and to see whether there is a link between how they were feeling about their work at these points and their work values. (The exercise on stresses and strains has not been included in the seminar guidelines because it is probably better to do a more detailed assessment of difficulties at work in a 1:1 rather than a group setting.)	Chapter II. Copy the work values cards and have scissors and envelopes.
20 mins	Stage 1 self-assessment	**Exercise 2: skills/achievements** See Chapter 2 for instructions. **How many examples?** Working in pairs, the trainees should analyse one work example and one non-work example.	Chapter II. Trainees foundation portfolio.
10 mins	Stage 1 self-assessment	**Putting the Stage 1 exercises together** Once the trainees have worked through the values and skills/achievements exercises, encourage them to draw out a heraldic shield, divided into four sections: Work values/interests Skills/stressors Ask the trainees to put a few bullet points in each of the four quadrants. Refer to example in the book. They can write a personal motto if they like. (And if they want more self-assessment exercises, direct them, for starters, to the Hopson and Scally book included in the resources list in Appendix B.)	Chapter II.

Time	Activity	Teaching notes	Resources
15 mins		**15-minute break**	
30 mins in total, including the exercise	Stage 2 career exploration	**Introduction to Stage 2** The next stage is to explore different career options to find out two things: 1. Which particular career pathways are most likely to match the trainees' skills, interests, values etc. 2. Given feedback from their educational supervisor and/or Director of Medical Education, the trainee needs to consider whether the option(s) they are interested in seem to be realistic career choices. **Other points to show** • Adequate career exploration takes time. • Stage 2 is not carried out in a vacuum – rather, Stage 2 follows on from Stage 1. • So the trainee can use the summary exercise from Stage 1 to generate a list of specific issues to be explored in their specialties of interest. • The clearer the trainee is about what is important to them (Stage 1), the more targeted and relevant their Stage 2 research can be. • Trainees will have to augment their reading about different options with talking to people – at various levels of seniority – who are currently working in this specialty. Without this, it will be difficult to ascertain whether the career is going to match their core work values, skills, interests, etc. • There may well be some to-ing and fro-ing between Stages 1 and 2. So, for example, something that the trainee finds out as part of their Stage 2 research might cause them to re-think some aspect of their initial self-assessment.	Chapter III

Time	Activity	Teaching notes	Resources
	Stage 2 career exploration	**Exercise 3: what resources are out there?** 1. The resources list at the end of chapter 3 contains a list of useful books and websites. 2. The MMC website can be used to access all deanery websites. The COPMeD site has links to all Royal College websites. Check these for relevant journals and events which give the opportunity to find out more about the specialty. 3. Check the noticeboard in the postgraduate centre for other useful information and details of local events. **Activity:** identify three career research tasks which follow on from the Stage 1 self-assessments that the trainee is going to undertake. The trainee should write these down, commit to a date for their completion and discuss the tasks with a colleague.	Chapter III
20 mins	Plenary	Recap that the purpose of this session has been to outline a framework (and thus provide questions rather than answers). Remind them that there will be further sessions, as part of the generic programme, which will look at Stages 3 and 4 (and will also look at post-F2 training routes in more detail). Encourage them to spend sufficient time on their career planning, rather than leaving it all to the last minute. Deal with any other questions.	

Appendix F
Workshop 2 – Introduction to career-planning seminar for F2 trainees

Introduction

The second workshop is for F2 trainees and should be run early in their F2 year as it covers application forms and interviews. The session should last three hours to ensure the material is covered adequately The workshop should be run by a clinician with experience of helping trainees with their career decision making and who has been involved in recruitment and selection to posts. An outline session plan is as follows:

- Purpose of the session and introduction: 5 minutes
- Brief review of the four stages: 10 minutes.
- Stage 3-decision making: 30 minutes
- Stage 4 application forms: 45 minutes
- Break: 15 minutes (this can be timed to suit local arrangements)
- Stage 4 interviews: 50 minutes
- Plenary and questions: 25 minutes

Workshop plan

Time	Activity	Teaching notes	Resources
15 mins	Purpose of the session and brief overview of the four stages.	Explain the four stages: 1. Self-assessment. 2. Career exploration. 3. Decision making. 4. Plan implementation. Introductory comments: a. The four-stage framework is one that applies to career decision making at any stage of one's career – it is not restricted to the current career decisions that the foundation trainees are facing. b. This session builds on the introductory session they may have had in their F1 year and specifically focuses on Stages 3 and 4 of the career-planning framework. It won't provide the trainees with all the answers, i.e. they won't be 'sorted' by the end of the session. Instead, the session aims to outline the preparatory	Trainees to have access to this book.

Time	Activity	Teaching notes	Resources
		tasks that trainees need to carry out prior to filling in their application forms and before a selection interview. c. The session will concentrate on Stages 3 and 4, and will only touch on the other two stages to set the context. d. Stage 4 (plan implementation) depends on the previous stages. If the decision rests on a firm foundation of self-assessment (Stage 1), career exploration (Stage 2), and how these match together (Stage 3), the trainee will be better equipped to write a convincing application form and provide good answers at interview.	
	Stage 3 decision making	Introduction to Stage 3 and an exercise.	
5 mins	Stage 3 decision making	**Introduction to Stage 3** People make decisions in different ways. Some mull over a decision for a while and then, on the basis of a gut feeling, become confident that one pathway is the right one for them. Others like to be more concrete in the process and draw up cost-benefit tables. Either approach is valid. Some points that you might want to raise include the following. • Ask them to reflect on past career decisions in order to identify what helped them reach a decision. Is this approach valid for their current career decision? • If they are considering post-foundation training in a specialty which is very competitive, it might be advisable for them to have a 'back-up' plan for a less competitive specialty. • Advise them to discuss their plan with a colleague, and also with their educational supervisor or the Faculty Careers Lead. Then, introduce them to the idea of the ROADS criteria.	Chapter IV

Time	Activity	Teaching notes	Resources
		ROADS – a systematic way of reviewing career decisions. **R**ealistic – are you being realistic about yourself AND about the demands of the job? **O**pportunities – have you given serious consideration to all the opportunities available? **A**nchors – have you built in the things that provide support in your life? **D**evelopment – do your choices fully develop your potential? **S**tress – have you considered those aspects of work that pose particular stresses for you? If you have time, take a career decision you have made in the past and review it with the group using the ROADS criteria. (It is better to use the facilitator's example than to ask for examples of previous career decisions from the trainees, as sometimes this can lead to quite a personal issue being unwittingly opened up in front of the group.)	
15 mins	Stage 3 decision making	**Lifeline exercise** This exercise can be used with both individuals and groups and is included in Chapter 3. **Exercise 1: Lifeline exercise** Ask trainees to complete their Lifeline, then ask them to split into pairs for the discussion. Ask the trainees to get together in pairs and discuss the following questions: 1. Which changes represented good career decisions? 2. Use the ROADS criteria to describe the ways in which they were good career decisions. 3. Were there any decisions that, in retrospect, were not so good? If so, use the ROADS criteria to describe the ways in which the decision turned out not to be so favourable.	Chapter IV. Blank paper

Time	Activity	Teaching notes	Resources
		4. Looking at their Lifeline so far, can they see a pattern in terms of what helped and what hindered any decisions that they have made in the past? If the trainee has made a decision about their post-F2 training, then they can analyse the decision using the ROADS criteria.	
10 mins	Stage 3 decision making	**Stage 3 plenary** Ask the trainees if they have any comments. You might also want to ask the trainees what they have learnt about themselves, in terms of how they approach the task of making decisions.	
5 mins	Stage 4 plan implementation	**Introduction to Stage 4** By stage 4 (which trainees need to reach well in advance of the time that they will have to fill out their application forms) trainees should know what post or specialty training programme they wish to apply for. The purpose of this stage is to write excellent application forms and prepare for interviews. Some trainees will already know what they are applying for but others may still be undecided. Either way, they can use the workshop to practise their techniques.	Chapter V
	Application forms	The timings for this session are: 10 minutes: provide an overview of the application process. 20 minutes: ask the trainees each to draft an answer to one question taken from the question bank, and then critique their answer in pairs. 10 minutes: share hints and tips.	Chapter V
10 mins	Application forms – overview	**Overview of the application process** Chapter 5 contains a flowchart which you can use to walk through the process. Do encourage trainees to assemble a CV, so they have all the information in one place, and stress the importance of asking their referees in advance. Bring out the key points from the	Chapter V

Time	Activity	Teaching notes	Resources
		information on initial preparation and golden rules. As a way of *preparing* to write answers for application forms, trainees might want to use the STAR structure. By this we mean the trainee could break down their example into: Situation/Task Provide a concise overview of the example you are considering using, ensuring that it is relevant to the question. Actions What exactly did you do? What were your role and contribution? What skills did you use? (This part will probably form the bulk of your answer). Results/Reflection What was the outcome? What have you learnt from it?	
20 mins	Application forms – exercise	**Exercise 2: application forms** Ask the group to split into pairs and to consider one question from the question bank detailed below. You may also wish to add your own suggestions as well. Trainees should prepare their answer individually and then working in pairs critique what they have written. In their critique, they might want to refer to the STAR acronym.	Chapter V
		Exercise 2: question bank 1. Give a recent example of a clinical situation in which you feel team-working could have been improved. 2. Describe your experience of clinical audit indicating clearly your own level of involvement and the clinical relevance of the audit. 3. Describe a difficult clinical situation you tackled well. 4. What do you consider the most challenging aspects of applying the GMC 'Good Medical Practice' to your own career?	You may prefer to develop your own questions.

Time	Activity	Teaching notes	Resources
		5. Describe your experience of clinical governance and indicate clearly your own level of involvement? 6. Describe your experience of working in multi-disciplinary teams, including your observations on the effectiveness of teamwork. You may give examples from both inside and outside medicine. 7. Describe how you deploy time-management skills in order to optimise your professional development.	
10 mins	Application forms – group discussion	Bring the group back together and ask them to share their thoughts about the questions they chose to answer. Try to ensure each pair contributes their ideas to the discussion. In this session refer to Chapters 5 and 6, to draw out the relevant points.	Chapter V
		15-minute break	
	Interviews	The purpose of this session is to give you an opportunity to discuss a selection of the questions foundation trainees might be asked at interviews. The timings for the session are as follows: 5 minutes: outline of the exercise. 25 minutes: for the exercise (in pairs). 20 minutes: reassemble as a group to share best practice.	Chapter V
5 mins	Interviews exercise – outline	Some key points about interviews: Most interviews will be structured and time-limited. There will almost certainly be more than one person present. If there is a panel, one member will be appointed as Chair, and is the person who is likely to welcome the trainee, introduce the other panel members, and outline the structure of the interview. Preparation is all-important as many questions can *broadly* be predicted in advance. So if trainees devote adequate time to pre-interview preparation, they should be able to improve the quality of	Chapter V

Time	Activity	Teaching notes	Resources
		their performance on the day. (Of course, trainees might still be asked some questions that they haven't considered before. But if a structured interview process is used, then at least trainees can be reassured that all the candidates will have been posed this particular question.) So how should trainees prepare? For starters it is helpful to realise that questions which are asked at interviews are usually divided into three broad areas: 1. Questions about you. 2. Questions about the job/specialty. 3. Questions about the wider context of health care. It is far better for trainees to refer to specific examples than to talk in generalities. The next exercise aims to give them a chance to practise structuring specific examples.	
25 mins	Interviews exercise	**Exercise 3** Ask the group to split into pairs and to consider at least one question from each of the three categories in Chapter 5 using the STAR technique they used for the application forms exercise. Check which questions are being covered so that you can ensure a reasonable range has been chosen rather than just the first two in each section. There is a selection of questions to choose from and you might wish to add some of your own as well.	Chapter V
20 mins	Interviews – group discussion	Bring the group back together and ask them to share their thoughts about the questions they chose to answer. Try to ensure each pair contributes their ideas to the discussion. In this session aim to draw out some overall general points and discuss interview technique.	Chapter V

Time	Activity	Teaching notes	Resources
15 mins	Final plenary	Recap that the purpose of this session has been to provide a review of the four-stage process, and then look in detail at Stage 3 (decision making) and Stage 4 (plan implementation). Encourage them to spend sufficient time on their career planning, rather than leaving it all to the last minute. Encourage them to identify sources of help, including local resources. Ask them to identify one career-planning task that they will commit to completing and that has come out of today's workshop. Get them to write this down, with a suitable time-scale, and then briefly discuss it in pairs. Deal with any other questions.	

Notes